W9-AOG-890

Questions, Claims, and Evidence

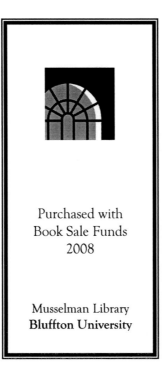

Questions, Claims, and Evidence

The Important Place of Argument in Children's Science Writing

LORI NORTON-MEIER
Iowa State University

BRIAN HAND
The University of Iowa

LYNN HOCKENBERRY
Loess Hills Area Education Agency

KIM WISE
Loess Hills Area Education Agency

HEINEMANN
PORTSMOUTH, NH

NSTApress
National Science Teachers Association

Heinemann
361 Hanover Street
Portsmouth, NH 03801-3912
www.heinemann.com

Offices and agents throughout the world

The National Science Teachers Association (NSTA), founded in 1944 and headquartered in Arlington, Virginia, is the largest organization in the world committed to promoting excellence and innovation in science teaching and learning for all. NSTA's current membership of more than 55,000 includes science teachers, science supervisors, administrators, scientists, business and industry representatives, and others involved in and committed to science education.

National Science Teachers Association (NSTA)
1840 Wilson Boulevard
Arlington, VA 22201

Library of Congress Cataloging-in-Publication Data
Questions, claims, and evidence : the important place of argument in children's science writing / Lori Norton-Meier . . . [et al.].
    p. cm.
  Includes bibliographical references and index.
  ISBN-13: 978-0-325-01727-3
  ISBN-10: 0-325-01727-1
   1. Science—Study and teaching (Elementary)—United States.   2. Science—Study and teaching (Middle school)—United States.   3. Technical writing—Study and teaching (Elementary)—United States.   4. Technical writing—Study and teaching (Middle school)—United States.   5. Language arts (Elementary)—United States.   6. Language arts (Middle school)—United States.   I. Norton-Meier, Lori.
LB1585.3.Q47 2008
372.3'5—dc22   2007049466

Editor: Robin Najar
Production: Lynne Costa
Cover design: Night & Day Design
Cover photographs: Lynn Hockenberry and Tracie Miller
Typesetter: Publishers' Design and Production Services, Inc.
Manufacturing: Steve Bernier

Printed in the United States of America on acid-free paper
12 11 10 09 08   VP   1 2 3 4 5

This book is dedicated to the teachers and students
who were willing to give the SWH approach a go.

Contents

Acknowledgments

It seems only appropriate when writing a book about science writing that we should use the very template that we advocate for science inquiries to express our gratitude to the many people who made this book possible. It all started with a question.

1. *Beginning ideas:* We had a question: "How does the Science Writing Heuristic approach work in the elementary classroom?" To answer this question, we had the help of many school districts, teachers, students, and administrators who joined us in this inquiry, asked their own questions about science and literacy, and pushed us every day to think deeply about teaching and learning.

2. *Tests:* The test was to examine the use of the SWH approach with classroom teachers in preschool through sixth grade. This work would not have been possible without the support of a Math-Science Partnership grant and the State of Iowa who supported the teachers and researchers to engage in this investigation.

3. *Observations:* We observed, interviewed, videotaped, analyzed, and took notes. We had dialogue and examined our data, which lead to new observations with an amazing research team including Murat Gunel, Recai Akkus, Sara Nelson, Sarah Trosper, Kyle Rasmussen, Elham Mohammad, Ryan Kelly, Ahmad Al-Kofahi, Bill Crandall, and Jay Staker. Over the years we have had numerous undergraduate students who have provided support to this project—managing data, scoring writing samples, transcribing, and analyzing: Micale Coon, Jessica Drey, Alicia Johnson, Kevin Jolly, Katie Raymon, Lisa Ryherd, Katherine Schnoor, Sara Ann Smith, and Ashley Titman. In addition, many preservice teachers participated in this project by providing an audience for SWH classrooms by reading and responding to penpal letters. Your thoughtful response over the years has made writing purposeful for children. Finally, a special thank-you to the many freshman honors mentees who chose to participate in the project as beginning researchers; your insight has been invaluable.

4. *Claims:* We made claims based on the evidence. Having the opportunity to "go public" with your claims and thinking is a key part of the learning process. Daily, we share our thinking with our colleagues, students, teachers, and friends at Loess Hills Area Education Agency 13, Iowa State University, and the

University of Iowa. We thank you for your continued support of our questions as teachers, researchers, and writers.

5. *Evidence:* Once the evidence was gathered, we reflected upon our understanding by writing. The results were overwhelming—when teachers are willing to re-examine their beliefs about teaching and learning and give the process a go, students and teachers are successful. Here we must thank the support of sixty teachers across the United States who read the first draft of this book, "had a go" in their own classrooms, and gave us extensive feedback to bring this revised draft to you. The field testing of the first draft was supported through a Teacher Professional Continuum grant (No. ESI—0537035) through the National Science Foundation. An advisory board has also provided thoughtful response and feedback on our efforts including Donna Alvermann, Sharon Dowd-Jasa, Todd Goodson, Kathy McKee, Wendy Saul, and Larry Yore. We thank you for your wisdom and continued "nudging" as we grow in our own understanding of teaching and learning, science and literacy.

6. *Reading:* We asked the experts—of course, the teachers and the students whose stories you will read in this book—but a special thank-you to Jan Westrum and Allyson Forney who read very early drafts of this book and provided insightful feedback about audience and style.

7. *Reflection:* Finally, reflection—in reflecting on what has made this project possible, we must thank our program assistants, Tracie Miller and Allison Donaldson. Your attention to detail, pep talks, humor, and ability to multitask has made this book an intriguing endeavor as you both reminded us daily of the important work we were doing. Also, a special thank-you to the Heinemann Team and Robin Najar for seeing the value in this project and providing ongoing questions to fuel the writing (and future investigations!).

And, with extreme gratitude and pride, we thank our families who create spaces and time for us to practice what we teach and continually encourage us to have a go with our many questions, ideas, and projects about teaching and learning.

CHAPTER 1

Questions, Claims, and Evidence

Examining Our Approach to Science Teaching and Learning

Voices of the Students in a Fifth-grade Classroom

I love the way that we do science now rather than how we did science in fourth grade because I learn more and I get to do more. I actually feel like I am smart.

I love doing science because we get to conduct our own experiments. I learn a lot more because if I do the experiment I know that it's true. Because how do I know if what they're saying is true? I like this better than using a textbook because I have to use my brain to think about the experiment and if you read a textbook— it just gives you the answers without thinking.

I don't like using textbooks at all. I like using the words *CLAIMS* and *EVIDENCE*. I'm enjoying the fact that I am using experiments all the time. I think you can learn a lot without using the textbook all the time and because I don't think your textbook tells you all the things you need to know.

Voice of the Teacher in This Fifth-grade Classroom

When I was approached to teach fifth grade it was with the condition that I would be responsible for teaching two sections of science. My heart raced. Science????? That "S" word??? I hated science all through my own schooling and had set up exploration centers for the science concepts when I taught kindergarten. Now I actually need to be knowledgeable about the different aspects of science. Could I do it? The jury is still out, but the process has generated enthusiasm and excitement for my students and myself.

From the voices shown in the previous section, it is difficult not to be intrigued by this approach to teaching and learning that has students and the teacher in this fifth-grade classroom abuzz. This teacher has been in the process of implementing this innovative science and literacy approach that incorporates asking questions, making claims, and gathering evidence into her teaching repertoire. For many elementary teachers, in the wake of the No Child Left Behind Act, we have seen science pushed out of our curriculum in favor of a focus on reading and mathematics. In this classroom and many others across the country, teachers are examining ways to link language and literacy experiences with rich science inquiry, and as evidenced in the previous statements, it is having a powerful impact on the learning of students in elementary classrooms and beyond.

About the Approach Used in This Book: The Important Place of Science Argument

So, what is this process that is supposed to help students learn science better, to encourage them to pose questions and explore their answers, and to do better on a variety of assessment measures? Why is there a need to move away from the traditional approaches to science teaching? We know that the number of students moving into science and science-based careers is decreasing—why? There are a large number of factors, but as teachers of science we have to ask ourselves what we are doing in our classrooms that fail to promote, encourage, and stimulate students to take up careers in science.

Traditionally, science laboratory activities are structured around the laboratory report format. Students are expected to engage in a format that outlines the hypothesis, procedures, observations, results, and discussion. Unfortunately, this format is typically used by scientists only to report their work to journals for publication. This is not what occurs in science laboratories. Scientists are involved in posing questions, making claims, providing evidence, debating with each other, comparing their answers with others in the field, and attempting to look for patterns across their results. Scientific argument is at the very core of science activity. Having completed this process of argumentation, scientists then prepare their written reports for publication.

While there has been much work done on examining the strategies required by teachers to be successful when using inquiry, two areas of concern still exist. The first is the lack of emphasis on argumentation, and the second is the limited or almost nonexistent focus on language use and its relation to science learning. In elementary classrooms, there is an additional concern that science has been pushed out of the curriculum to provide more time to focus on reading and mathematics. To address these concerns, we would like to share with you a new idea or, rather, an approach to thinking about science that offers a variety of language and literacy learning opportunities paired with quality science inquiry. We call this an approach because it is not a kit or a slick little strategy or a new scripted program. Instead, it is a *lens*—a lens to examine what we do and how we structure learning opportunities in our classrooms. Throughout the coming pages, we plan to share with you this new lens for you to try out and to expand your understanding of teaching and learning, science, and literacy.

About This Book

This book is designed to give you the opportunity to explore the approach in your own classroom. With this in mind, the book is divided into three sections. The first section is aimed at providing some *background* examining teaching, learning, and writing. The authors believe it is essential to recognize that using this approach requires more than simply gaining a new strategy. We need to review our understanding of what learning is. Is it transferring information? Is it about constructing knowledge? Most important, we need to examine how our view of learning matches up with our view of teaching. This section examines our perspectives on learning and teaching and how these perspectives are critical for using the approach. The section finishes with a discussion on language, focusing on writing and its essential function in learning science.

The second section deals with the *implementation* of the approach. We have structured this section around the student plan for the approach. We begin in Chapter 5 with an exploration of the art of questioning and how to help students to ask good questions. In Chapter 6 we describe how good questions lead to the gathering of evidence. Chapter 7 deals with making claims and how to assist our students in analyzing and reflecting on their investigations and research. Chapter 8 takes the reader to the conclusion of the process where students reflect on their learning through the summary writing experience as well as a discussion about assessment. The intention of this section is to introduce the teaching considerations required when using the approach focusing on student learning in elementary classrooms (K–6).

The third section is framed around how to examine *teaching practices* and a review of *frequently asked questions*. Chapter 9 begins by providing an overview for planning your first unit and introduces a performance matrix that we have used throughout our studies when working with teachers. The intent is to provide guidance to teachers so that they can examine how well they believe they are implementing the approach. Chapter 10 deals with frequently asked questions posed by teachers and an overview of the research findings related to this approach over the past nine years.

Particular features of this book include many opportunities to read the stories of teachers and students in elementary classrooms as well as pose some challenges to engage the reader through the pages of this book. Each of these special features is set off in the text. These features include:

TEACHER'S VOICE: We believe the teacher's voice is essential to our work, and we have included their stories of joys and struggles, aha moments, and frustration points to help describe in detail the implementation of the approach.

FROM THE STUDENTS: Throughout the pages of this book, we will provide examples of student writing and the student voice from inside classrooms, prekindergarten–sixth grade, to help you get an insider perspective on student learning.

CHECK THE EXPERTS: Just as there is a place in the plan for the students to read about what others say, we have provided many links to other research, helpful websites, and resources for further reading and investigation.

BOOKS AND TOOLS: Over the past nine years, teachers and consultants who have worked with this approach have developed a variety of tools. Many of these tools are provided throughout the book to help you get started in implementing your own unit. We also will share a variety of books and ideas that fuel our own science-literacy investigations.

HAVE A GO: Finally, the book concludes with the "have a go" appendices. These featured activities are for the reader to try in and out of the classroom setting to engage in active learning experience around the implementation and examination of the approach.

We have written the book with guidance from a group of teachers who have been using the approach over the past three years. They have provided insight and critical comments and made sure that we as authors are focusing on the children and the realities of the classroom. We thank this group.

Who are we, the authoring team of this book? We are teachers, too—teachers who continually examine our own teaching in science and literacy with children and adults. Thus, in the pages of this book we will use a collective "we" as we stand with you asking questions about how children learn, how we orchestrate learning opportunities, and how we continue to ask questions, make claims, and gather evidence—the same actions we are nurturing in our students.

We hope you enjoy the book and take up the challenges that are presented in the following pages. Taking the time to work through some of the suggestions and advice has been very beneficial for all the teachers and students who have been using the approach. In the wise words of another fifth-grade student, "I think using this system is more fun and easy. Learning with experiments is a way to understand. I don't know why anyone wouldn't want to do it. What are you waiting for?"

Building Our Knowledge Base for Questions, Claims, and Evidence

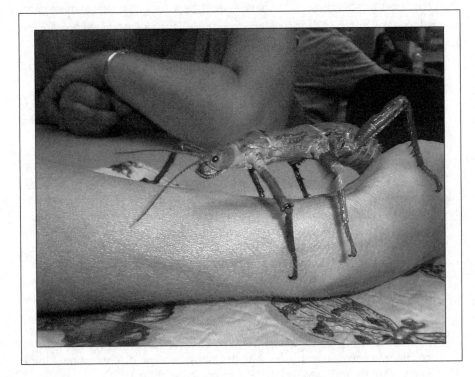

Figure I.1 *Interesting photograph to stimulate dialogue*

The picture above was displayed in a first-grade classroom. The teacher asked the students on the first day of school what they would need to be prepared to look at the photograph as scientists. When Ms. Thompson (throughout the book we will use pseudonyms for all teachers and students) turned the picture around, oohs and ahhs rose loudly from the twenty-one first-grade students. Then the dialogue began.

"What IS it?"

"Well, my claim is that it is some sort of an insect."

"It kinda looks like the grasshoppers I get in my backyard!"

"Whoa, but this one is big!"

"Do you think we get these in IOWA?"

"Do you think it *bites*?"

"Of course it bites, but I am not going to gather any evidence on that!"

"I wonder if when it bites you it itches like a mosquito bite."

"Why are the legs so long?"

"Do you think it makes a noise like a cricket?"

"How can you tell if it is a boy or a girl?"

"How fast is it?"

"I wonder if it can fly."

The teacher sits back gently in her chair and listens (and smiles). In this one introductory activity, she is learning so much about what her young students know about science and language. They demonstrate the ability to ask questions, make a claim, and talk about gathering evidence. Interestingly, the first-grade students already know so much about the work of scientists.

What does it mean to be a scientist? Students in a sixth-grade classroom began the year with a writing challenge. The teacher asked the question, "What are the essential characteristics that scientists need to have to do their work, and which of these characteristics do you possess?" Three of the students' insights are presented here for examination.

Scientific Characteristics

A scientist can be anyone, even a first grader. Anyone who asks questions, learns from her senses, and notices details is a scientist. Scientists have a passion for learning about certain topics they are studying.

The scientific characteristics of a scientist are: #1—Scientists are patient. They can't rush or they will just ruin the task they are doing. #2—Scientists are educated. They need to be smart and need to know what to do in frustrating situations. #3—They are open-minded. They can't get distracted by things around them. #4—They are curious. They want to know why something does what. Those are four things all scientists do or need to do to be a great scientist.

The scientific characteristics of what I think I have are: #1—I'm hard working. If I start something I always try to finish it; I always stay on task. #2—I'm observant. I like to look closely at things around me, mostly nature. #3—I'm determined. I always believe I can do it; a lot of times, I don't, but sometimes I do. #4—I'm creative; I always include extra detail. Those are four scientific features about me.

There are a lot of factors required to be an exceptional scientist. Not only do you have to have the brains, but also the motivation and determination. I think I have all of the traits required to be a successful scientist.

—By sixth-grade scientist #1

Characteristics of a Scientist

There are many different types of scientists. For example, there are scientists who study animals, plants, medicine, and so much more, but most scientists have a lot of the same characteristics, characteristics such as intelligence, curiosity, and creativity.

I think scientists are intelligent people who know a lot about what they specialize in. They study every detail so they know everything about that one subject their researching. A good scientist should also be curious, because they are always trying to figure out new things, and if they weren't curious they would never find the answer to a problem. Scientists are creative because they are always looking for new ideas and creating new things.

Some scientific characteristics I might have are I'm creative because I think of new ideas all the time. I might also be a good scientist because I love animals and I would really enjoy helping to find new cures for them. I have a strong will and don't give up on something that I really care about.

Scientists have very similar characteristics, but they also have their own characteristics and I think everybody has a little scientist in them—even me.

—By sixth-grade scientist #2

Becoming Albert Einstein

There are three characteristics that I think all scientists should have. One of the characteristics is patience. Scientists should be patient. If a scientist isn't patient enough, they may give up too soon and never know their experiment actually worked. Scientists should be creative so they're able to think outside the box and try new and different things. They have to be very accurate and precise too. If they aren't accurate and precise in their methods, they may make a mistake that could change the results of their experiment.

I think I have several characteristics that would make me a good scientist. I have lots of patience. For example, I never give up on an idea unless I'm sure it won't work and I've tried it more than once. I also am very thorough. I take time to read and follow all the directions so I don't miss any important steps. Lastly, I am very organized and neat. When I read and do the steps for my idea, I make sure I do it in a very organized and neat way. Being a scientist is a very hard job. It may seem easy but it takes a lot to do the job right! Who knows, if you are patient, creative, accurate, and precise, you may be the next Albert Einstein!

—By sixth-grade scientist #3

What is it that these three young writers know about the work of scientists? Are they correct? Do we see any misconceptions present in their thinking? This beginning writing sample has provided their teacher with important insight into the thinking of her students in relation to science, writing, and what the students see as some of the important attributes they will bring to her classroom. Throughout the year, the teacher will help to question and expand their definition of scientist and the work of science.

This leads to an important question, "What exactly is our role as teachers in the learning of our students?" How do we help our students to question their thinking, make claims, back up that thinking with evidence, and be prepared to defend their thinking with peers using scientific argumentation? In this section, we will examine what it is that we know as teachers about learning (Chapter 2), teaching (Chapter 3), and how writing is an essential element in science inquiry (Chapter 4).

Learning Is About Understanding
(Theory and Practice)

Teacher's Voice

What is learning? As a veteran teacher I thought I knew the answer. At the first summer workshop I realized that learning was a topic of confusion for many of us. In fact we spent several hours discussing the topic, and many of us still left without a clear understanding. I've decided that maybe that confusion was okay. We as teachers are still learning—taking what we already know, adding new information, and fitting it into our own schema.

The first year of using this new approach was definitely a learning experience for me. I spent way too much time focusing on the process. I worried about filling out the template, getting forms sent in, preparing the videotaping, and doing a number of other trivial things. It was very frustrating for me because I've always loved teaching science.

The second year has been much better. I've had a change in thinking. My focus now is more on the actual learning that is taking place. We tried a concept map for the first time. I asked the kids to write down all they knew about the topic of heat energy as well as questions they might have. I was amazed at the amount of yellow sticky notes that were hung on the board and some of the questions that the kids had. As I read the notes I could pick out children who already had some understanding of the concept and those who didn't know much about it. Organizing the questions gave us a focus for what the students wanted to learn about heat energy. To me this is one of the most powerful parts of this process. It allows the children to be in charge of their own learning. It's become clear to me that only the learner is in charge of his learning.

It's thrilling to me as a teacher to see children excited about science. I will continue to question, discuss, listen, write, and reflect . . . all parts of helping me negotiate my understanding of how science and literacy should work in my second-grade classroom.

—Second-grade teacher

One of the most common areas of discussion when talking with teachers is about their role in the classroom. As educators we focus a great deal of attention on what we do on a daily basis to engage learners. We are constantly striving to improve our teaching in the classroom. From the preservice teacher to the experienced teacher, we all see our role as helping students to learn, assisting them on their journey to become independent readers and writers, and helping them become important and valuable members of society. We all work hard at developing our skills so we can assist students in learning and see that growth from the beginning to the end of the school year. An important question that we need to deal with is, "How much time do we spend on exploring the second component of what occurs in a classroom, that is, learning?" An equally important question is what do we really understand about the term *learning*, and how is this related to teaching?

What Is Learning?

Philosophers have been discussing learning for many years, and many ideas from their work can help us understand the process of learning and teaching. In one such example, Strike (1987) discussed the idea that

people are active in learning or knowledge construction; this line of thinking is disputed by only a few behaviorists. Strike's idea sets the stage for our thinking over the last fifteen years and underpins the basis for all the curriculum reform documents brought out in the '90s. The National Science Education Standards (NRC 1996) place great emphasis on the need for students to be active learners, to inquire and be curious about science, and to communicate their understandings to others. Constructivist learning theory has been the buzzword in science education and is often used within these curriculum documents.

What is cognitive theory? If one builds from Strike's idea, then we accept that cognitive theory focuses on the broad concept that each individual is active in a process of constructing knowledge. Many different theories have been put forward under the broad umbrella of cognitive theory, such as information processing, radical constructivism, social constructivism, interactive constructivism, and developmental theory to name a few. It is not our intention to discuss these in detail, but rather we will consider some of the terms that are often brought forward in discussions on learning. If asked to draw a concept map of what we understand about learning, what would be some of the terms that we would need to write down? Think back to the educational psychology books, and yes, we do remember names such as Piaget, Vygotsky, and others, but what did they say? Try to see what you can remember—how many terms can you remember?

Here are a few terms that might appear on your list:

❖ Learning

❖ Understanding

❖ Conceptual frameworks

❖ Assimilation

❖ Accommodation

❖ Disequilibrium

❖ Conceptual change

How are these terms connected and what do they really mean? Let's start with *learning* and *understanding*—these are not the same. Within the education psychology community, learning is defined to be when somebody has gained some knowledge; this could be a skill or some content material. Understanding refers to the ability of the learner to transfer her knowledge to new and different situations. The authors of the National Science Education Standards recognized this difference when they suggested that the central goal of science teaching is having "students learn scientific knowledge with understanding" (p. 21). These differences in terminology are important because they begin to shape what we understand and practice in the classroom.

In the following discussion we will focus on understanding, that is, the building of conceptual frameworks or schemas, which a learner can use in any situation. Our current understanding of knowledge storage is that we have conceptual frames, or schemas, in which to store knowledge. A conceptual framework is viewed as an interconnected *web* of knowledge built around a single concept. For example, if we say the word *fishing*, then automatically we have a series of images, words, and ideas that are connected and define our individual understandings of fishing. These understandings differ between people; for example, people who live in desert-type climates with no familiarity of frozen lakes and streams would be unlikely to incorporate concepts of ice fishing in their conceptual frameworks. Every individual has a unique conceptual framework. That is, every one of us stores knowledge in a unique web based on our background knowledge and environment. Even though we might all receive the same message or content knowledge, we interact with this knowledge in slightly different ways because our conceptual frameworks are not identical.

What does it mean to *interact* with this knowledge? Cognitive theories of learning are based on the notion that a learner has to *negotiate* meaning. In other words, a learner has his or her own knowledge that will interact with the new knowledge to increase the total amount of knowledge stored. In addition to negotiating her own understanding of the meaning of the new knowledge on an individual level, the learner has to negotiate the meaning across the various groups of people who will interact with the learner. For example, when studying the concept of force, the student has to negotiate his own understanding about the word and the meaning the teacher has given to the word and concept, as well as the meanings relayed by family members, peers outside of the classroom setting, and other various texts and images such as books or movies. In each of these contexts the meaning of the word *force* can vary, and the individual has to be able to negotiate a meaning of the word depending on the context. A parent can force him to clean his bedroom or a popular movie states "may the force be with you," but this does not mean the teacher's concept of Newton's first law is being applied.

When the learner is asked to read a textbook about force, we are asking her to negotiate meaning from the text. She has to negotiate between her own knowledge and what the text is telling her. Similarly, when writing the learner has to negotiate meaning between what is known and what he believes the audience can understand. It is important for us to understand that this process of negotiation is constant—knowledge is not simply passed from one person to another. While we might believe that we have provided a clear and simple explanation of a concept, each learner has to go through a process of negotiation to arrive at an understanding. Students can take notes and give us back what we want to hear, but that does not mean that is what is stored in long-term memory. This concept of negotiation of meaning was one of the important contributions of Lev Vygotsky (1978) to our understanding of learning.

If learning is about negotiation of meaning, is there a particular process that is required that moves from a student learning the concept to constructing an understanding of the concept? Since the mid-'80s science education has been guided in great part by the idea of a conceptual change process. Successful negotiation of meaning requires that the learner construct a richer version of the concept; that is, the student's conceptual framework is different from when he she first started.

Teacher's Voice

When we consider learning and how children negotiate meaning, this intriguing example happened in one classroom:

"Mr. Sanders, I don't think that grass is a plant," states Andrea, age seven, on a bright, sunny day during the third week of school in her second-grade classroom in a Midwest suburban elementary school.

Mr. Sanders kneels down to Andrea's eye level and replies, "Well, Andrea, I think you just made a claim! Would you like to share your claim with the rest of the class?"

Andrea nods her head, and Mr. Sanders calls the students to the carpet.

As the students gather around the teacher's feet at the carpet, Mr. Sanders invites Andrea to share her claim. She begins, "Okay, class, my claim is that I don't think grass is a plant."

The room erupts in chatter when one small boy calls out, "Hey, Andrea, what's your evidence?"

"Well," she thinks as she replies, "I read in that book over there that all plants have roots and I have never seen any roots on grass, so my claim is that grass can't be a plant."

Once again the room is abuzz. Mr. Sanders has an idea.

"Hold it here. Andrea has made a claim and has provided a bit of evidence to support her claim. Let's see here . . . okay . . . if you agree with Andrea, why don't you come stand on this side. If you disagree, come stand over here."

The children hustle and chatter, but when all are situated, one small boy is the only one opposed to Andrea's claim.

"Hector," states Mr. Sanders, "you don't agree with Andrea?"

"No, I don't. I KNOW grass is a plant, I don't know about the root thing," he thinks.

Another child from Andrea's side calls out, "We need to take this to COURT!"

Hector, still thinking, calls out, "I've got it! You know when you pull out a stick of grass, there's that white part at the bottom. That has to be the root!"

A chorus of "nos" rose up from the class.

"Okay, okay," Mr. Sanders attempts to provide direction. "So, we have two claims and it appears we need to gather some evidence. What could we do to investigate this question—is grass a plant with roots?"

Jason says, "Well, I think we better go to the playground and pull up some grass!"

Hector adds, "Yeah, and let's put the evidence in a bag so we can examine it when we get back in the classroom."

So the students get organized and head to the playground. They are amazed as they pull up a blade of grass and examine what could be considered a root. Andrea says, "Okay, this grass may have roots, but that grass over there doesn't."

With Andrea's comment, each child chooses a different spot from around the school to pull up a small sample for examination. They return to the classroom, and the children share their samples and conclude that Andrea's claim is wrong—grass is a plant.

"I still stick with my claim," states Andrea. "I know the grass at my house does not have roots, so grass cannot be a plant." Mr. Sanders encourages her to gather some evidence at her home tonight and report back to the class.

The next morning, a sullen Andrea walks into the classroom. She slowly lifts her bag with a clump of grass, makes eye contact with the class and Mr. Sanders, and simply states, "I'm speechless."

What Is Meant by Conceptual Change?

To begin, we all have some basic understanding of a topic, however disconnected it is; conversely, the only framework that we have to look at a topic that is completely foreign to us is the framework that exists in our heads. For example, if we do not have a chemistry background and someone talks about equilibrium, we do not have any idea what this concept is or what it represents. However, we know what the term *equal* means or what an equals sign represents. Thus, we tend to look at the topic of equilibrium based on our concept of equal, which initially would appear to have no connection to chemical reactions and equations. To build a rich understanding as opposed to rote learning about the concept of equilibrium means that new knowledge coming in has to be connected in some manner to our existing conceptual frameworks. The question becomes, "How do we build on our existing conceptual frameworks?"

Any decision to change a framework is the decision of the individual. It is the individual who makes a choice to add, delete, or keep unchanged this framework. We as teachers do not have any control of what goes on inside anyone else's head. As teachers we can control the environment but not the cognitive activities of an individual. Thus, for an individual to change what he believes, he needs to make some decisions about how satisfied he is with what he knows when he begins to examine a new topic or idea. Such words as *disequilibrium, dissatisfaction,* and *perturbation* have been used to describe the condition that learners will undergo when faced with something that is new or different to what they currently believe. To change existing schema, learners need to feel as though what they currently believe will not adequately address the problem or the topic with which they are currently engaged. Simply having an external source telling them that they are wrong is no condition for achieving change. Evidence of this is the lack of success we have with students who cannot seem to understand an idea no matter how many times as the teacher we teach and review.

Thus, the first step in getting the learner to undergo some conceptual change is for her to begin to be dissatisfied with what she currently believes. Does this mean that she will automatically adopt the new knowledge that is "fed into the system"? If it were that easy, our jobs would be so much simpler! Who then makes the decision about how valid the new knowledge is that the individual deals with at any given time? Again (we will keep reiterating), it is the *individual* who makes decisions about the value of the new knowledge. Conceptual change theory uses the terms *plausible* and *intelligible* to describe the conditions required by the learner. These conditions refer to the concept that the new knowledge not only makes sense but also appears to be true or have value. Why do learners have difficulty grasping science concepts when we as teachers have made a very logical presentation? Has it made sense to the learners? Why do advertisers have so much success in selling their products? Mainly because they appeal to the perceived needs or wants of the buyer who then believes that what is being presented is true. How many weight-loss programs or exercise equipment have been sold because buyers believe what is being said applies to them and the claims therefore are true?

Teacher's Voice

Creating opportunities for children to share, develop, and expand their conceptual frameworks in a fourth-grade classroom:

When I begin a new unit, to assess prior knowledge, I give each student a pile of sticky notes. Each student puts one word on each sheet about something he or she knows about the topic. Some students know many words and ideas, and others will know very little. This activity generates vocabulary and concepts known about the topic. I then have the students bring their words up to the board to share with the class. If a student has an idea or word that has already been used, his or her note is placed on top of the others. The students feel a sense of belonging and validation that they had an idea that one of their classmates had too. We continue in this process until everyone has had a chance to share his or her words. Then, as a class, we use the words to create our concept map. I like to use sticky notes because as ideas change or more knowledge is gained the ideas can be moved around. I also leave the map on the board during the entire unit and use different colored notes to reflect the new ideas. The students are very excited to change their concept map once new knowledge is gained. Using the colored notes was a real "wow" for the students. They would look at the board and say, "Look at how much we learned!"

Once the first draft of the map is made I have students—either in groups or individually—generate questions they have about the concept. The questions are written on chart paper and placed around the room. We talk about each question and decide if it is a researchable or testable question. If the question is testable, a lab is created. If the question is researchable, then the students have the opportunity to use nonfiction text. This can be done as a class reading activity; in addition, as the answers are found individually by a student, that student can write the information on a sticky note and place it next to the question on the chart paper. These are then shared and discussed with all students.

Concept maps are a great place to post vocabulary words for the concept you are studying. During the electricity unit one of the fourth-grade boys in my class knew that electricity liked water (these were his words). Later through our lab and reading he learned the word *conductor*. We went back to our concept map and replaced *likes water* with the word *conductor*.

As a class we are constantly referring to the map and revisiting it to reflect new knowledge. As teachers we need to remember the map is the students' concepts, not ours. At first there probably will be misconceptions and wrong ideas that hopefully will be understood and addressed as the unit progresses.

Having made a decision that the new ideas are valuable and make sense, will the learner then use them? There is not a definite black-and-white answer to this. The conceptual change theory uses terms like *fruitful* and *feasible* to explain this phase of learner use related to the new or adapting concept. By this theorists mean that learners will use the new ideas if these ideas begin to solve problems for them that their old ideas did not. Does this mean that the new concepts become part of the learner's conceptual framework? Current thinking suggests that this takes time and repeated use across a number of different situations. In essence, there is a competition going on between old and new thinking in relation to conceptual change theory. If the new concept can solve more problems or be applied to more situations more often, then it will become the dominant one within the learners' framework asking the question, "How does this new knowledge fit into existing frameworks?"

Historically, and still today, there has been rich discussion about what occurs in the process of learning. Two terms put forward by Piaget (Piaget and Inhelder, 1969), *assimilation* and *accommodation*, attempt to provide an explanation for what occurs. In terms of the change to existing frameworks, the question revolves around the degree of change needed. This becomes important in using the Piagetian terms. If the learner is adding new knowledge to the framework that is not radical, but rather extends or strengthens the framework, then we tend to say that this knowledge is *assimilated* into the existing framework. By this we mean that the learner is not making a significant change to what he believes. However, if what is required is a completely new *branch* of the framework to be developed, we tend to use the term *accommodation*. The learner is required to accommodate a different branch of the framework that will be in competition with the existing branch dealing with the particular phenomena or problem. It is important to understand that accommodation is not a spontaneous thing. It does take time and repeated use of the new branch of the framework. Again, we will reiterate: *The learner is the one making the decisions about the individual's own framework and how much repeated use is required to have final acceptance of the idea.*

In summary, understanding is about an individual engaging her conceptual framework in an attempt to use new knowledge across a broad range of situations. Learners are trying to negotiate meaning or make meaning from the situations that they face, and the only real "filter" they have is their conceptual framework.

Teaching and How It Connects to Learning

To continue this discussion, we draw on a quote that builds on this body of knowledge, although it was first used in the '60s. David Ausubel (1968), a psychologist, reminded us that the most important aspect of our work in education is to find out what the child knows and begin there. We personally believe that this quote should guide all teaching. If learning, leading to understanding, requires that individuals engage their conceptual frameworks and extend these, then teaching must be oriented to these frameworks. We need to remember that teaching does not occur in isolation to learning.

If we as teachers have no control over what is going on inside an individual's head, then we have to be able engage with learners in ways that make their knowledge the center of the conversation. How long have we heard that as teachers we tend to pitch our lesson at the middle group? That way we are reasonably confident that we can get to most of the students. In general, didactic teaching tends to be the passing of information from the teacher to the students. That is, we as teachers act as gatekeepers of knowledge. We parcel out what we think the students can handle at any given time. We judge our success by making sure that when we question students, they can give us back what we have given out. While we are not suggesting that there is not a place for sharing or giving out information, we will discuss later how that should be done differently to what is generally the process in many classrooms.

Teacher's Voice

From a preschool unit on "Animals Have Basic Needs," which explores the question: Who is in control of learning?

Animals such as mice, rabbits, birds, guinea pigs, chicks, ducks, and fish were all around the room during the course of the unit. After a few weeks of taking care of the animals, we began a discussion on what students had been observing. One student said, "Our bunny needs food and water every day. We know this because we put food and water in his bowls in the mornings and then the food and water is gone the next morning." Another student said, "Ducks needs food every day, too. We feed them all the time. As soon as we put food in the bowl, they eat it. They also need water. As soon as we put water in their bowl, they begin drinking it. Sometimes they swim in it." Similar conversations continued among the students as they talked about the different animals.

I was feeling pretty good about their realization that food and water were needs that animals have. Then a student said, "Our fish needs food, but he doesn't need water." I'm thinking some student will voice the fact that fish do need water. However, no response came back from the students. My traditional teacher mode came to the surface, and I said aloud, "She says fish need food, but do not need water. What do you think?" A student answers, "She's right. Fish don't need water."

Then, I picked up the fish bowl, swirled the water around that is obviously in the bowl, and asked "Fish don't need water? Think about where fish live." Students were silent for a moment before a boy in the back raised his hand. Knowing my question pushed this student in the right direction and the announcement that fish need water will be made, I called on the boy. He stood right up and very proudly said, "She's right! Fish don't need water."

So much for my thinking that I have any control over what students learn! However, I do have control over where to lead students next in hopes of clearing up the misconception that fish do not need water.

If learning is about having to negotiate meaning, then teaching ought to provide learners with opportunities to do this. As teachers, the first thing that we need to do is determine how much students know about a topic. We need to play with a number of different strategies that allow students to put out in the public forum what they know about the topic. There has been much written about such strategies. Some strategies are Predict, Observe, Explain (POE) activities, which require learners to predict what will happen, observe the activity, and then try to explain the result. In most cases, they struggle with explanation or have to elaborate nonscientifically acceptable explanations. Another activity that is used extensively in the elementary area is the KWL activity. Students are asked what they Know about the topic, what they Want to learn or wonder about the topic, and on review, what they have Learned about the topic. More details and descriptions about how to help students activate prior knowledge will be shared in Chapter 5.

The difficult thing for teachers from this point is how to plan for the rest of the unit. We tend to plan a unit in a manner that is based on how we think the unit should go or as it is outlined in the teacher's manual. An important question to consider is, "How can we plan a unit when we do not know what the students know or where the students are in their understanding?" Planning a unit without first finding out what the students know is a futile endeavor. Those teachers who have taught for many years tend to build intuitive understandings of what troubles students have with a topic but that does not mean that we know what this year's students are like or what their knowledge is in relation to any given topic or subject.

"Yeah, but that means that we will have twenty-five different kids with twenty-five different ideas!" This is an intriguing excuse; however, we know from research that students tend to cluster around some common scientific misunderstandings. While each student is an individual, from a conceptual viewpoint there tend to be only a few major groupings within a single class. Any one of these scientific misunderstandings can be used as a starting point of a unit—remember, it will be where some of the students already are in their understanding. Students as a whole can then begin to appreciate that their knowledge is going to be challenged and expanded on through the activities and experiences in the classroom.

Building on these ideas, planning needs to focus on the concepts or big ideas that frame the unit. *Learning is about understanding concepts, thus teaching must be about concepts, NOT content.* To understand any concept we need to build in the relevant content. We need to challenge students' conceptual understandings, not their rote learning of content. Examples of planning using big ideas will be discussed in the next chapter. By asking students to focus on the concepts framing the topic, we provide opportunities for students to match how they learn with how they store knowledge. Much of what is currently done in terms of information transfer strategies is that by the end of the unit the students are supposed to have an "aha" moment—the point at which the students have been able to build the content into some form of conceptual understanding. For the many students who never come to terms with science, a major factor is that they never get to understand how all these ideas and content fit together. We need to match how we learn with how we teach.

Teachers share moments when they witnessed the development of conceptual understanding in their students:

Teacher 1: When we were talking about heat and the kids decided at lunch that they could continue to show how heat transfers. They put their butter container in the mashed potatoes and showed how the butter melted. Then someone said, what would happen if we took the lid off the container. Would it slow down the melting process? What if we poked holes in the lid? If we put the butter container into the peas would we have the same results? The kids said it would melt slower because there is air around the peas and not the same amount of surface would be touching the container to melt the butter. They put a spoon into the mashed potatoes and could feel how the handle seemed to get warmer as the heat moved up. Playing with food at lunch can be a learning experience!

Teacher 2: During a unit on different animal groups, I had a student who was able to connect the ideas we had focused on during two or three different activities by explaining how one animal could belong in several different groups at the same time and didn't have to be in just one group (for example, a pig could be in the "farm" group for habitats, the "four legs" group for appearance, and the "plants" group for type of food). This idea was eye opening for some other students who had the idea that each animal belonged in only one group and were having difficulty deciding where the animals should go.

Key Understandings

There are two important major cognitive ideas that we need to focus on within science classrooms. First, every individual's learning is an activity that is undertaken by the individual for which we as teachers have no control. Learning is an activity that is controlled by an individual. Second, knowledge is stored in long-term memory as conceptual frameworks, not as separate content knowledge points. The function of learning leading to understanding is to develop and enrich one's conceptual frameworks. *The key point to remember is that the individual learner controls learning.*

CHAPTER 3

Teaching So Children Can Learn

Teacher's Voice

At our final summer workshop, the teachers were asked to write a metaphor for their teaching before and after the science literacy project. Below, a sixth-grade teacher shares how her thinking about teaching has changed through this process of implementation:

Before this project:

My teaching was a desert with no visible forms of life. I dispersed most of the information and assumed my students were so thirsty for knowledge in that barren oasis that they would naturally just soak up every drop of information I had to give.

After this project:

I now know my classroom is much more of a jungle with energy and activity bursting from every location. Students are much more engaged in thinking, discussing, finding out the reason "why" than ever before. I get to be much more of a jungle cat, lurking, waiting to pounce on student uncertainty and push them into discovering more. Even when I don't know the answers, I know it will be okay and we can work as a team to find clarity. The students now provide the energy and the life toward building their learning.

When discussing our teaching, we often refer to it as "orchestrating opportunities." With this in mind, we delve into a discussion of just how we bring this notion to life in our classrooms. So, if teaching is to be aligned with learning as discussed in Chapter 2, what does that mean for us as teachers of science in elementary classrooms? If we follow the two key points that a learner is the only person who controls what goes on inside her head, and that knowledge is stored in conceptual frameworks, what do we understand about the pedagogical skills that need to be developed? What do we need to change from what we are doing now? What are the key areas that we need to focus on to create an environment where this learning can occur? We believe that there are five essential skills: determining the big idea(s) for the topic, planning the topic, finding out what students know, questioning, and performing group work. These areas are discussed in this chapter. However, we first highlight the important concept that teaching is separate from management. Teacher-centered, teacher-controlled classrooms are designed *first* to manage the students and *second* to promote learning. Learning and teaching are not about managing students—although good management strategies must be in place to implement cognitively based learning strategies. However, they are two different concepts: Poor management leads to student and teacher frustration and poor learning. Ask yourself the following: (1) Have students engaged in answering their own questions and constructing knowledge for themselves? (2) If so, when have you had major management problems?

Determining the Big Idea(s) for the Topic

As teachers, we typically base our unit planning on the material that has to be addressed within any one topic. Many teaching manuals attempt to make this easier by highlighting all the major content in bold lettering within the text. The emphasis from textbook publishers is on making the curriculum material *teacher-proof* so that it will be delivered correctly to the children. Thus, the unit to be taught is basically framed around the content highlights and chapter summaries. The idea of having the material linked in a conceptual manner is considered covered by asking the learner to complete the concept map at the end of the chapter, which is already laid out with a fill-in-the-blanks approach.

From the Students

In the concept map featured in Figure 3.1, a third-grade classroom demonstrates their thinking in action. Rather than a fill-in-the-blanks concept map, this "busy" writing sample illustrates the students' use of words and how they are attempting to negotiate meaning. And this all started with a blank piece of paper!

Figure 3.1 *A concept map developed by a third-grade classroom*

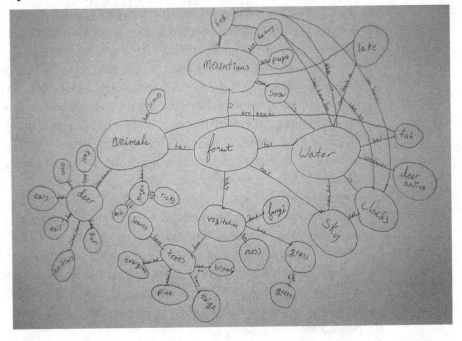

National and state standards are based on creating curricula that center learning on the big ideas of the science discipline area. How do we translate these into our classrooms? The single most important task is to determine the "big ideas" that are to be dealt with in the topic or unit. What is/are the major concept(s) that the students should leave the classroom with at the completion of the unit? Think carefully—not the content items, not a list of facts or vocabulary words, but rather the big idea that the students can use wherever they go. What is the organizing idea that frames the topic?

When you determine this one idea that you want students to grasp, then this idea frames the conceptual understanding that you want to build on with the students. This is not an easy task! When we started working with teachers and asked them to undertake this task, one teacher, after much effort, said that he had narrowed the number of important concepts down to sixty-four! Thinking that this might be a *little* too many, we were able to negotiate the final number down to two. How do we get started on this challenge of identifying the big ideas?

Teacher's Voice

Finding the "big idea" is never an easy endeavor:

Kindergarten Teacher: I had done a tree unit nearly every year of my teaching career. I LOVE THIS UNIT! My little students and I go on walks and identify trees by their leaves, study the parts of a tree, and the like. Then, one summer as I sat down to work with one of the graduate students on the project, he asked me, "So what is the big idea?" I was stumped. He continued, "Tell me, why is it important that my young son learn about trees?" After some thinking, I replied, "Well, they are essential to people's lives! They provide shade, food, and shelter and clean the air." I realized the big idea has just fallen out of my mouth. But, I can't tell you it was easy. It took me time to realize that the "cute" leaf identification activities that I have known and loved for so many years may not be helping my students to understand the "big ideas" of trees and science. Sometimes it is just as tough for us teachers to give up our prior notions about what is important to teach.

Sixth-Grade Teacher: Every year, our curriculum required the teaching of a unit on woodlands. We hated that unit and so did the kids. We could not find any way to go beyond memorized facts and the reading of information. So, we would save that unit until the end of the year, and if we couldn't get to it—oh well! Then, we had the opportunity to talk about the unit with a biology professor from the university. He reminded us that the fundamental question of biology is "same or different?" Also, he gave us permission to stop worrying about all the "right" names and setting the students loose as if they'd landed on a new planet and were scientists trying to determine the amount of biodiversity in that habitat. He recommended a trip to a beautiful state park, which is only a mile from our school, where we could mess around with the biodiversity focus. It could be narrow (for example, just trees) or it could be broad (anything they can find), but the point would be for the students to attempt to perceive as much diversity as they could. Wow, a BIG IDEA and a way to make this boring unit come to life in an active experience for sixth graders!

The most important step is to stand back from the teacher's manual or kit that you are using and examine *your* understanding of the topic. Let's begin with one of the science units that you typically teach. If you have to tell your spouse, partner, or close friend (any classroom outsider) what the idea about the topic is that you want students to take with them, what would it be? Now go to the reference material and check your understanding. We say the word *understanding* here because these are the ideas that apply to a range of different situations. These are not the dictionary definitions; these are what *you* have as *your* understanding. We have to be able to view the topic or unit as a concept framework with a central core idea(s); otherwise, we struggle to implement cognitively based strategies and make sense of what we are learning.

What does this look like? In the following sections we have provided two examples, one from biological science, the other from physical science, to show you what we mean by the big idea of a topic.

Example 1—Biological Science

A topic that is often covered in schools is ecosystems. Teachers need to ensure that students are exposed to a range of different biomes such as the tundra, rain forest, and taiga. Also, each of these systems has to deal with biotic and abiotic factors. Each of these different biomes must deal with nutrient and energy cycles. Is there a single common concept that links these knowledge points and ideas together? When a student leaves your classroom, what is the concept that you want him to have about the topic? An organizing concept for students to understand is that any ecosystem is a system in balance. All the different biomes to be studied have the same basic structural features—decomposers, producers, and consumers, with cycling abiotic factors. Regardless of the biome, these things exist, and all biomes are attempting to maintain a balanced system.

We often hear, "Yeah, but this is obvious!" If it is so obvious, why are textbooks, teaching manuals, and various kit materials not organized around this idea? Why do teachers insist on treating the different biomes as distinctly separate from each other? They are separate in the types of plants and animals that exist in them, but conceptually they are all the same.

Example 2—Physical Science

Topics covered in physics at school include magnetic forces, gravitational forces, and electrical forces. Each of these is covered in separate units, and they are not seen as connected. However, they are linked by the single idea that force decreases with distance. Yes, the quantities are different—magnetic, gravitational, and electrical forces are different types of force. However, as the distance increases, the effect of the force decreases. The important concept for the student is that, regardless of the type of field being studied, the force will decrease. Students can then organize their understanding around the big idea and see that each of the examples studied has its own unique properties, but they are each linked via the organizing framework.

Having determined what the big idea is for the unit, students and teachers must create a concept map that fits together all the unit's content in the manner in which it is connected to the big idea. The concept map is a representation of how the knowledge of the topic is stored in long-term memory. The big idea becomes the organizing frame for all the content associated with the idea.

From the Students

Concept mapping is a powerful tool to understand student thinking. Teachers have used this strategy in a variety of ways. However, when we began our process, we had to make certain that we all had the same understanding of what a concept map was and how to create one. The next two pages contain two examples from students. The first one is not what we would call a concept map; it is a semantic web. A concept map often begins at the top or center and should have linking words on the lines between each bubble and idea. In fact, a well-created concept map should be able to be read from top (or center) and follow down the set of connecting words and ideas to create a sentence. Not only does this help students articulate their thinking but it also teaches them important lessons about the mechanics of the language. We will discuss creating concept maps with our students more in Chapter 5.

Figure 3.2a *Example of a student semantic map or web (no linking words)*

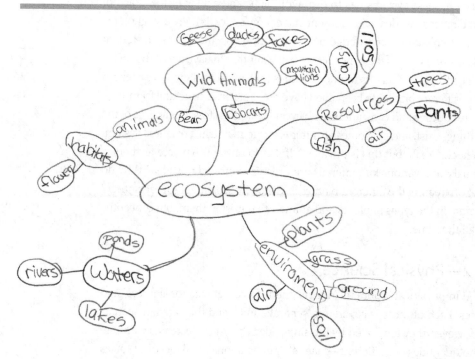

continues on next page

Figure 3.2b *Example of a student concept map (with linking words)*

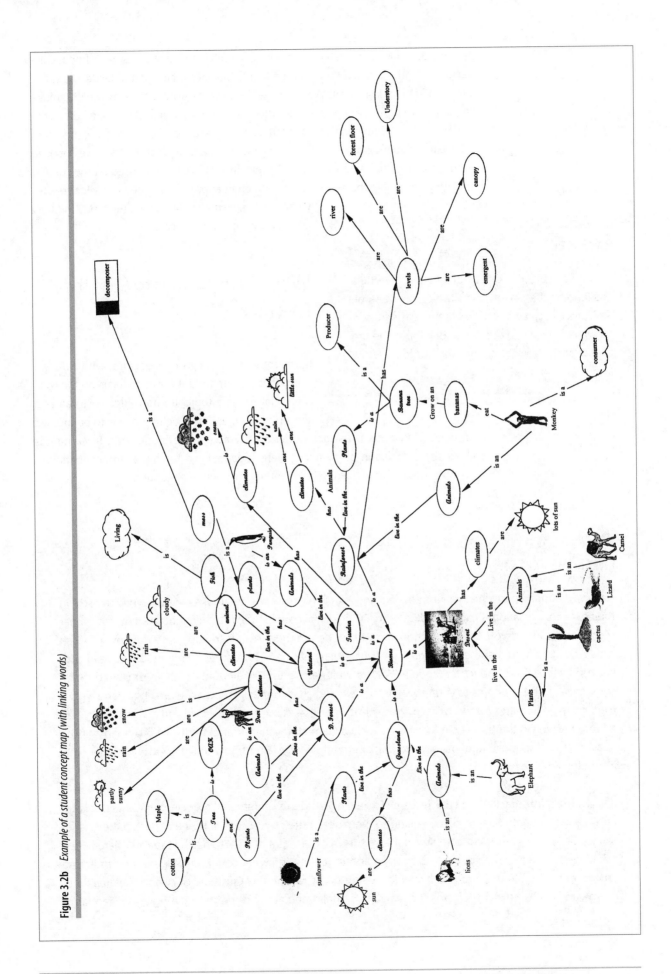

For each of the topics studied in school, a unifying idea or ideas exist. In our conversations with teachers, they indicate that this is the single most difficult concept to pinpoint in planning a unit. We have tended to view learning as a linear path, thinking that if we lay out the pathway for the students, they will follow. Somehow at the end of the unit, having laid out the path for students, the conceptual view of the world will be unveiled magically and the aha moment arrives. As teachers, we have not dealt with the conceptual framework of the topic. Instead we have focused on the content and, thus, reversing the role requires a different approach. We need to ask ourselves what it is that we understand about the topic, and how this matches up with theory.

HAVE A GO!

Finding the big idea of a unit can oftentimes be a challenging task. In Appendix B, we provide some assistance to get started by examining the following questions: (1) What do I know about the big ideas? and (2) What should my students know about the big idea?

Why Is It Important to Get the Big Idea(s)?

If we are going to align our teaching with how we learn, then it is important for us to focus on the concepts that frame a topic. If knowledge is stored as a conceptual frame, then teaching needs to be focused on helping students construct a scientifically acceptable framework. If learning is about the negotiation of meaning, then students need to engage in negotiation of concepts, that is, they need to be *constantly* engaged in negotiating.

CHECK THE EXPERTS

Have you noticed that when you introduce a new word to your students, it takes them a while to use it in their own conversation? Pearson and Cervetti (2005) discovered in their research that students must hear the teacher use the word in conversation many times before they are able to add it into their own speech acts. We have found that the development of vocabulary has been supported by many strategies including the Picture Word Induction Model (PWIM) developed by Emily Calhoun (1999). In one third-grade class, she asks the students to create visuals for new and challenging vocabulary words by taking a photograph that illustrates the word. Then, these photographs—along with the word and the dictionary definition written on the back—are hung on the classroom clothesline that extends from one end of the classroom to the other. Students have to think in multiple ways about how to make the vocabulary real for their fellow classmates.

Also, a fifth-grade teacher used this research to help her students understand the scientific concept of preferred environments. She began by talking to them about their bedrooms at home. What do they prefer to have in that space? What colors? What furniture? Carpet? Lighting? When the students shared their thinking, the teacher then began a discussion about beetles and what could possibly be their preferred environment. Would they prefer hot or cold? Wet or dry? Grass or dirt? Cluttered or clean? The questions, claims, and evidence were rich, and the teacher was delighted at the students' growing understanding.

Students who do not have success in science often fail to come to terms with the language of science. A major problem is that they are unable to play the memory games associated with answering multiple-choice, fill-in-the-blank, or other such types of questions. By changing the focus to the big idea(s) of the topic, we are able to provide all students with an opportunity to change from the memory game to building understanding of a topic. Students move from a list of disconnected vocabulary words to negotiating meaning of the words in relation to the big ideas of the topic.

A critical component of student-centered learning strategies within science classrooms is for students to be engaged with scientific argument as a way to negotiate meaning. Students need to debate and argue about the big ideas of the topic as central elements in the negotiation process. By working through claims and evidence for a topic, the students will be able to move past a simple list of words to construct rich justifications for their understandings of the topic.

Planning the Topic

The focus on big ideas does cause a change in how we plan a topic. Planning is not about how many textbook pages need to be covered in a single lesson or period, but rather, it should be focused on structuring lessons to allow opportunities for students to build connections to the big ideas. Does that mean that there is a need to throw out all the activities that have been used previously? No! Does that mean that the textbook is not to be used? No! It does mean, however, that we have to take a different orientation toward this material. Remember, we are not focusing on what we, the teachers, know. We are focusing on how to help students build understanding.

It is not a case of the teacher giving the information to the students so they can give it back to us (this effectively means that we are really testing how much *we* know!). If we are going to implement inquiry-based strategies within our classroom, we need to have the students active in exploration and evaluation of ideas.

From the Students

Second-Grade Teacher: In our plant unit, the class wanted to do some projects in small groups. The groups could come up with their own projects, or we (as a class) could make a list and they could pick one of those. I was amazed at the projects they came up with. We made a sheet and the groups picked out what they were going to do. Two groups came up with their own topics and went to it. All groups were very involved. Some showed experiments, some made A–Z books on plants, and one group went out on the school grounds and drew the plants they saw. They each split up the area so they could see the common ones and then group them. Then they looked everywhere to identify the plants. This lead to further grouping as they then organized the plants to other places they can be found, based on the information they read. From there, they discussed the common features of plants. This information was presented to the class and the conversation grew.

The first step in planning is to determine what activities will assist learners to focus on and investigate the big ideas of the topic. Consider whether you are using the activity to demonstrate theory or as an opportunity for students to construct knowledge from the activity. Traditionally, we have used laboratory or hands-on activities to demonstrate the knowledge that we have covered in previous lessons; or, we have used the activities to set up for coverage of material for the next series of lessons. The questions that need to be asked are numerous: (1) How does this activity promote investigation of the big ideas; (2) If students were able to pose questions about the activity, would they be able to derive claims and evidence from the activity that would help them construct an understanding of the big idea; and (3) How many activities do we need? The answer to this last question will be determined by how students respond to the activity. If they grapple with an understanding of the big ideas quickly, then the number of activities will not be many. However, if they struggle, then more opportunities for engaging with the big ideas will be needed. There is no set formula for determining the number of activities to be used.

Having selected a series of activities that you want to incorporate in the unit plan, next consider how to reshape these activities to promote student-centered engagement. Remember, we as teachers do not control what goes on inside a learner's head; we control the learning environment. Thus, we need to reorient the activities to provide opportunities for students to pose questions about the activity, complete the activity, and use scientific argumentation strategies to justify their conclusions.

Examples of change could include:

1. Not providing the blank shell of the data table to be used. How do we get students to understand which observations to do and what data to collect if we constantly provide fill-in-the-blank activities? Students should be working through what data to collect and how best to represent this data.

2. Require small-group discussion of the activity and pose questions *before* they are able to undertake the activity. Rather than telling the students what to do and how to complete the activity, students need to wrestle with trying to understand what the activity is asking of them.

3. Instead of groups doing exactly the same quantities, provide opportunities for variation of the quantities, examples, and so on. Therefore, when the whole class is discussing the results, they are required to think more broadly and look for patterns. Furthermore, the students will have to account for variations and provide strong justification for the generalization being constructed. This method is much more powerful than simply having the answer confirmed by the teacher.

When planning the unit we have to be flexible. While we may plan ahead what we as teachers believe is the most important sequence—understanding that it may not be the one that the learners want to undertake—we must remain flexible in our planning. In the process of continually negotiating meaning with students, the appropriateness of the sequence that you have planned might need to change. What you have planned may not challenge or build on where the students have gone in their thinking. This does not mean that the activities you have chosen are not valuable; it means that the teacher does not solely determine the sequence of their use. In planning for the unit and then working through planning for individual lessons when teaching the unit, we must always ask the question, "How will this activity support the students in constructing their understanding of the big idea?"

Does this mean that we cannot give students information? No! If students reach a stage of not having knowledge of the activity or concepts being explored, then we need to provide them with some information. We can, and should, build in opportunities for information sharing with the students. However, unlike traditional forms of science teaching, we cannot simply keep giving information. It has not worked well for us before, so why would it be any more successful than previous efforts? Thus, when planning information-sharing sessions, it is essential that opportunities be built in for students to make connections between the new information and the big ideas of the unit. Remember, students will be trying to negotiate their understanding of what is being said. Teachers need to make this negotiation public and plan opportunities for public negotiation between new information and the big ideas. We need to know what the students are doing with the new information and if they are connecting what we have shared with them to what they currently believe about the topic. Just because we give information does not mean that students will store the information in the manner for which we intended.

Having planned for activities and information-sharing throughout the unit, we also need to plan for some form of activity that will enable students to pull all of the big idea(s) and content knowledge together. This does not mean that they should copy the vocabulary list from the end of the chapter or the bold words throughout the chapter, or complete the fill-in-the-blanks concept map. In all of our research projects, we have worked with teachers to use some form of writing-to-learn activity as an end-of-unit summary activity. As will be discussed in the next chapter, writing-to-learn activities are activities that require students to move past recall knowledge to explain what they understand to different audiences using different types of writing. This practice can include such activities as writing letters to local government officials, writing explanations to younger students, or writing brochures for the local tourist industry. This summary-writing activity is not simply an exercise in giving students practice at using the correct words. It is a *learning* activity. This activity is just as powerful a learning activity as any of the others discussed previously. *Teachers need to plan some form of activity that requires students to summarize their understanding through the negotiated meaning-making process of writing.*

The final and critical piece of the planning process is the assessment component. By constantly engaging students in negotiation of meaning, we can continually assess them throughout the unit. The question then becomes: How do we do an end-of-unit assessment? There are many ways to do this including writing opportunities (we will explore this in the next chapter), practical activities, interviews, and tests. We would like to focus on tests as these are common throughout all schools; that is, end-of-unit tests are the predominate mode of assessment. Traditionally, most tests are based around multiple-choice questions, fill-in-the-blanks, matching words, or problems for which there has been a great deal of practice during class time. How do these types of questions focus on students' understanding? Most of the questions that are traditionally used are focused on recall knowledge. In other words, students are playing memory games. If we are trying to align our teaching with how we believe learning occurs, should we not be trying to align our assessment to learning as well? If the focus of our teaching is to have students build conceptual understanding of the topic through negotiation of meaning, should teachers not provide forms of assessment that require students to display that same kind of thinking? Why would we want to use assessment items that require only recall (low-level thinking) when we have focused on requiring students to be cognitively active in constructing knowledge and requiring them to use high levels of thinking? Therefore, when planning for assessment we teachers need to match assessment to learning.

Teacher's Voice

When it came time to pre- and posttest my second-grade students on the plant unit, I knew I would need to do something very different to allow each of my second graders to show his or her unique understanding and learning through this unit. Not a single one of them came in with the same knowledge as the others. So how could I let them demonstrate what each knew and learned? Well, I decided to let them show me. I put out all kinds of art materials—chenille stems, a variety of paper, and so on, and I asked them before the unit and after the unit to create a plant with all the parts. Then, they were to present their plant to me and explain what they had created and why. How intriguing! And what changes did I see in their understanding of plants from beginning to end! Best of all, no two plants looked the same, but all of the basic parts and functions of the plant were present. It became another opportunity to explore our common theme and big idea: "Plants have similar parts and functions." Throughout the unit, with each experiment and ongoing discussions, students were continually changing features to their designed plants.

In all of our research projects, when working with teachers we have taken the approach of including extended response questions on the end-of-unit tests. These are questions that require students to connect to real-world situations, to explain to other people certain components of the big ideas, or to display how the content knowledge is connected to the big idea(s) of the topic. They don't have to study for these questions. As we will discuss in the following chapters, students in our approach rarely ever do end-of-chapter summaries and end-of-chapter questions from the textbook. While we have heard from many teachers that they always do this type of testing, all the teachers in our research projects have struggled with this facet of the teaching approach. For example, in one third-grade classroom, we began with two questions: (1) What are the three states of matter? (2) How can matter change? These two questions gave us very little insight into students' thinking. Essentially, it was rote memorization. We started over and came up with two new conceptual questions: (1) Jim and Susie were sitting outside eating Popsicles on a hot day. Jim says his Popsicle is a solid. Susie says hers is a liquid. Who do you agree with and why? (2) A glass of water sits outside for an entire year. What changes might we see happen? These questions provided a plethora of detailed information about students' thinking from pre- to posttest, giving specific insight into each student's developing conceptual framework. Instead of expecting that each child would parrot back the same three states of matter and the way that they change, the new questions required them to make claims and back them up with evidence from their own experience and experimentation. Constructing these test questions takes practice, both in framing the question and in deciding how to mark the question. Remember, it is not only about the exact answer—the question is also about the thinking that the students display.

Teacher's Voice

Third-Grade Teacher: Science in the past was not something I felt very comfortable teaching due to it not being an interest of mine. Things changed after being involved in the program. I have learned teaching practices that benefit not only science but other subjects as well. I think the one thing that stands out is the importance of understanding what each student's background knowledge is prior to teaching the unit. That became very evident to me just recently. I was amazed at the reaction students had to the pretest they took on the skeletal and muscular system. As the students were taking the pretest, they were very frustrated at their inability to answer many of the questions. They knew they were about to enter a subject with very little background knowledge and that bothered them. What was so surprising was that the pretest actually motivated my students to learn. They wanted to know what a joint was and what moves your body. I found the key to learning that day—MOTIVATION! Last year I got my feet wet with the matter unit. I found myself learning some things that I didn't realize about matter before. My students laughed at their pretest answers after having a very successful posttest. It was neat to see them amazed at their own learning. The performance levels of their child also surprised their parents.

Find Out What the Students Know

After the planning is complete, what is the next step? A line of thinking that has guided us, and framed a great deal of science education since the late '60s, is one from David Ausubel (1968), who wrote that it is essential to find out what students know and begin there. This thinking underpins the very essence of cognitive learning theories as they are applied to schools. If we believe that learning is an action completed and controlled by the individual and that the individual constructs knowledge, then the starting point of any teaching and learning activity has to be the students. Thus the question becomes, how does what we have planned fit with what the students will personally and socially construct? What assumptions do we make, or have we always made, about student knowledge and what they bring to the classroom?

We have heard and/or been involved with educators who tell us about aiming for the middle group of students in the class, to make sure all our goals and objectives for the lesson are clearly laid out, and to have our questions planned out well in advance. All this preparation work is about the teacher—we need to make sure we are prepared and ready and can complete our job of teaching. Where do the students fit in? Are they simply empty vessels for us to fill? Are they eagerly waiting for us to pass on the message? Where does learning fit into the act of teaching? Traditional science teaching would appear to treat these two entities, teaching and learning, as two separate commodities. Teachers teach. The students' job is to learn.

We need to see that learning and teaching are not separate acts, and, thus, we need to merge our teaching with how we believe learning occurs. Therefore, we need to find out what students know *before* we start the unit. If we are going to help students build understanding of a topic we need to know what they understand at the beginning of the topic. *It is not about what we know; it is about what the students know.* Rote recall of information is replaced with the goal of building understanding that can be applied in a number of areas.

With this in mind, the first act of teaching for a new topic or unit is to implement an activity that enables the teacher to find out what the students know. There is a large range of activities that can be used. As mentioned in Chapter 2, a POE activity (Predict Observe Explain) is where students are asked to *predict* the outcome of an event and then *observe* the event (for which their predictions generally do not hold). They are then required to *explain* the resulting outcome. Another commonly used activity is the K (know), W (want to know), L (learned) chart. Generating a concept map at the start of a unit is another way to explore students' initial understanding of the topic. We have had students read newspaper articles and debate the topic as a starting point. It does not matter what activity is used, provided it gives students opportunity to voice what they know about the topic.

Teacher's Voice

The following are some ideas teachers have used at the beginning of the unit to understand what children already know about the topic:

Preschool Teacher: In the preschool and kindergarten ages, give the students lots of time to simply "play." Students need opportunities to manipulate objects, talk to each other about these objects, and listen to language from others. For example, during a unit when my big idea was "objects have different properties," I used sponges as a vehicle for learning. The first day of this unit consisted of students working in groups to play with sponges of all different sizes, shapes, weight, color, and textures. Students also had water, cups, tubs, and blocks of wood.

My role in gathering ideas of what students knew was to simply wander from group to group and listen to what students were saying. It's very easy at this point to gather language and knowledge from students as they interact with each other. I also listen closely for questions students are asking each other, as these give me powerful information into what students know and what they do not know.

Second-Grade Teacher: When I was doing a balance and motion unit, I was trying to decide how to do KWL a different way, so I grouped the class into groups of three and had them come up with topics to determine what they knew. One group decided to do a play using characters riding bicycle-like vehicles. One student was on a bike with training wheels, one on a regular bike, and one on a unicycle. They presented this play to the class, explaining how they had to balance differently on each bike, which brought in the concept of motion a little, too.

Having obtained this information about students' prior knowledge, what do we do then? How do we use the plan that we started to build? Remember that planning is about deciding the activities to be used and the content needed to address the big idea(s) of the topic. The sequencing of these activities and material occurs after we have found out what the students know, not before.

Teacher's Voice

Planning a unit for this approach is different than traditional lesson planning. First, I identify the big idea with help from my district standards and benchmarks. Then I make a concept map to reflect my own understanding of the topic. I write a pre- and posttest, focusing on conceptual understanding. I collect ideas for activities that could be used in the unit and assemble books and magazine articles relating to the area of study. I think about writing activities that will support the science learning.

Once I have started the unit, my planning is done on a day-to-day basis rather than planning for an entire week or the whole unit at once. This method allows me to select activities and plan lessons based on what the students need at the time.

Keep in mind that we are focusing on helping students build understanding and can shape the sequence of activities so that students are constantly challenged and required to negotiate understanding. This is not easy to do and requires experience at attempting this sort of planning. The plan will change for each class that you are teaching, and it will change every time the unit is repeated because we do not have the same students each year. The plan does not have to be radically different, but we have to be flexible enough to match the sequence of activities to the group of students that make up each year's class.

Questioning

The previous sections related to the planning of the unit. The emphasis on planning can never be overstated. When moving past the planning stage into interacting with the students, two critical teaching skills are key—questioning and group work. However, a major caveat must be addressed. A focus on learning requires good management strategies. Traditional, didactic, and information transfer strategies are centered on maintaining classroom discipline. In this form of teaching, management comes first and learning is a by-product. There is a need to separate management from learning and teaching. As teachers we need to ensure our classroom is safe, students are respectful and well behaved, and the environment is conducive to learning. This is not about teaching and learning; this is about creating an environment that enables students to be involved in activities that are aligned to how they learn. Having created what has been termed a nonthreatening learning environment, we can now implement teaching strategies that are focused on how we believe learning occurs.

We all understand the importance of questioning students—that is what we do in our classrooms every day. What is different about questioning if we adopt student-centered learning strategies? First, we can no longer play "guess what is in my head" games. Students are used to this game. They see us as teachers searching for the right answer or for the correct words. Having found the right words, phrases, or answers to a problem we immediately move on; that is, once we have the correct answer that is in our heads, then we assume that everyone else has the same idea and, thus, we can move onto the next question. We are taught to use the IRE method—teacher *initiates* a question (what is the third planet from the sun?), a student *responds* with an answer (the earth!), and the teacher *evaluates* the answer (well done, Jonathan). Do we wonder why students in our classes are reluctant to answer questions? Why should students take the risk when they constantly lose in the game of "guess what is in the teacher's head"?

If playing "guess what is in my head" games are not the way to go, then what is? Student-centered learning strategies are about *the teacher finding out what is in the students' heads*. If learning is about negotiating meaning, then questioning is a critical element of that process. We need to use questioning as a strategy to find out what students are thinking, challenge their ideas, and debate the outcomes of the inquiry activities that students are involved in so they are working to develop their individual conceptual frameworks. We have to encourage and support the students to make public what their reasoning strategies are and how they have constructed their arguments.

What are some of the essential skills that we need to use? First and foremost, *we need to get out of the way*. We talk far too much. When we ask teachers to view videotapes of their teaching they are horrified about how little time is spent in giving students a voice. We need to pose a question. In most cases, we should try to pose questions that require students to move beyond recall and think through possible solutions to arrive at an answer. When students answer a question, two things have to happen. First, we have to stop making judgments about the answer; that is, we have to stop letting the students believe that we are the arbitrator for deciding whether the response is correct or incorrect. One way of doing this is to constantly ask the question "why?" every time a student responds. Watch the dynamic in the classroom change. Second, to encourage dialogue, we need to allow the group to pass judgment on the answer. Instead of the teacher passing a judgment, the class should participate and come to consensus.

The important point to remember when questioning is that you are trying to determine what is in the students' heads and why they have arrived at these ideas. Negotiating meaning requires us to challenge students to account for their ideas and maneuver them toward the scientifically acceptable ideas.

Does this mean that we cannot ask recall questions? No, of course we can. However, these should not be the *predominant* mode of questioning. Even when asking these questions, still ask other students to confirm the answer. It takes time and practice to change our habits, so we need to continually spend time practicing these different techniques.

We often hear people tell us that they have been doing inquiry teaching for many years. When we dig a little deeper, what they mean is that they have their students doing activities—activities that are set by the teacher, with the direction of the questions being controlled by the teacher, and "guess what is in my head" games being the dominant questioning format being used. We keep coming back to the idea that *we have to change what has been our traditional mode of operation. We need to choose a simple starting point and practice*. It is important to watch the change in your students. They will resist the fact that you are not going to supply the answer. They will complain that

HAVE A GO!

Where do we go to learn to ask better questions? How can I begin? Start with Appendix D where we explore how we can ask better questions.

you are not doing your job. However, what quickly becomes obvious is that the quiet students tend to find a voice because now they do not have to fear being wrong. The low-achieving students who do not play the memory game well can now become involved because the questions are not about right or wrong but about the big ideas. The dynamic of the classroom will change.

Another area of change that we need to have when talking about questioning arises when dealing with the situation of information sharing. That is, when students have arrived at an impasse, we need to provide information often called *just-in-time* instruction. What we mean by this is that direct "information sharing" teaching occurs when the students need it. Traditionally, we seek to ask questions that confirm for us that the students have the information that we have transmitted to them. We use the IRE pattern of questioning, searching for the correct answer. As soon as we have the answer—generally from the students who always answer correctly—we move on to the next point that we want to make certain that they understand. We often ask the question, but does everyone understand "X"? Nobody says anything to the contrary, and so we assume that they all know it. We know that not all the students understand, and even if they answered that they were unsure, what would we do? Repeat our explanation or try to find a better explanation? The important idea that we need to remember is that it is the *students* who are going to make the connection between what they know and what you have told them. Our questioning needs to challenge them to explain how they are connecting the bits of information.

Teacher's Voice

We had spent several days studying and testing changes in states of matter. Students were looking for an explanation of how water got on the outside of a glass of cold lemonade. Where did the water come from? Claims and evidence had been shared. Students were reading to learn what the experts say when one of the girls suddenly jumped up and announced, "We are all wrong!" She continued to share her reading and gave a clear explanation of her new understanding.

From the Students

In the following examples, third-grade students share their developing understanding of concepts related to matter. In this classroom, after several investigations, the teacher had the students pause to create shape poems related to their learning and connect them to what they had learned about matter. In the following examples, we see how the students selected something from their world (hamburgers, cats, or the fact that many children in the school were ill with chicken pox!) and engaged in the act of transferring what they understood about matter to these seemingly everyday objects. The artifacts give us an intriguing insight into their developing knowledge and understanding of "matter."

Figure 3.3a *Shape poems by third-grade students about matter*

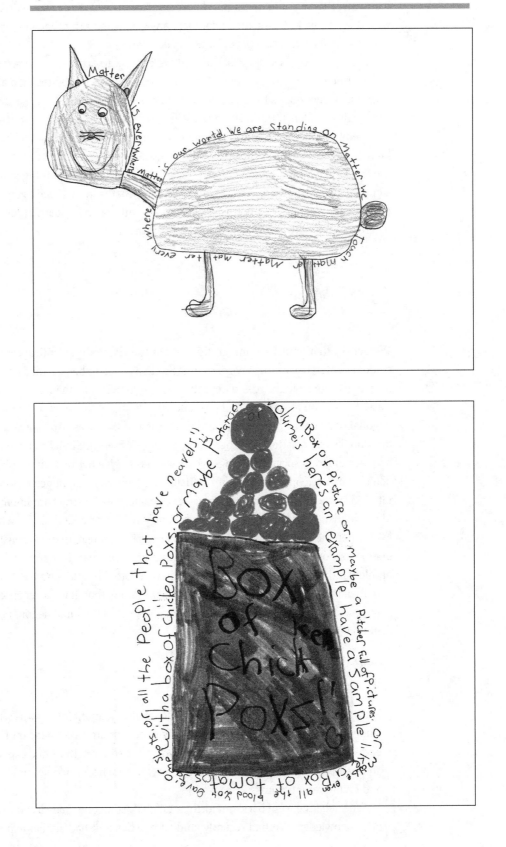

Now the simple question becomes, "How is what I have just talked about connected to what we have been dealing with in science?" Again the strategies discussed earlier need to be put to use in the classroom. Ask students to discuss with each other what they think; ask students to compare answers with each other—*use any strategy that requires them to explain how things are connected.*

There is no one set of questions that we can ask to achieve success. There is no predetermined series of questions that have been found to be better than another for learning for success. As teachers, we need to build questioning strategies that work in challenging students' understanding. When questioning students in our classroom we need to remember the overarching question that we must ask ourselves: Whose knowledge am I dealing with throughout this learning opportunity? Questioning is the single most important skill when using student-centered learning strategies. By stepping away from simply telling and playing "what is in my head" games, we can change the dynamics of the classroom into a nonthreatening learning environment where all students can engage with the subject matter.

Group Work

We believe that implementing group work in the classroom is critical for success in student-centered learning environments. Students need to be provided opportunities to negotiate meaning across different settings—individual, small group, and whole class. The reason for providing these different settings is that a critical component of negotiation is engaging in public understanding of the ideas. An individual student does not live in isolation from her peers, family, or friends. She is constantly moving between different social groupings where she has to give her thoughts, opinions, and beliefs. Such activities are part of her daily life. However, in science classrooms, we rarely give students opportunities to discuss, debate, and construct arguments for their ideas. Students are engaged in individual negotiation of meaning the whole time. Even when they are sitting in the classroom not saying much, they are constantly trying to work out how what they are being told fits into what they already know. The problem is that they rarely get a chance to have a voice in explaining what is going on with their thinking and how they have fit the pieces together. If we teachers constantly play "guess what is in the teacher's head" games, then individual negotiation by students is never challenged.

Teacher's Voice

Fifth-Grade Teacher: The most memorable science moment for me was when my students were sharing their claims and evidence for an experiment on how our body breathes. Each group had performed an experiment, the same experiment, and had written a claim and supported it with evidence. I had six small groups and four different claims.

The debating went back and forth until finally someone made a connection to prior knowledge. We had recently studied muscles and had similar experiences with that topic. A student said that maybe something was pulling the lungs. This sparked the attention of another student who piped up, "Muscles pull! Maybe it's a muscle." Well, as you can imagine this caused the room to be full of conversation once more. The idea of a third lung was also mentioned. Another student who said that he had never heard of a person having three lungs shot this down.

This was such an exciting science class. Sure, I could have just said, "Open your textbooks to page 123 and read about the diaphragm and how it is involved with your breathing." But would they have remembered this or even cared? Instead I had fifteen students leave school that day begging to have science class tomorrow to research and find out if they were right. I even had one student ask if he could use the Internet that night because he just had to know! WOW! Now that's learning at its best.

The function of group work is to promote the shift from individual private negotiation of meaning to public negotiation of meaning. We want students to make their ideas public in order to be challenged by their peers. Students will change their ideas more readily by this process than by us teachers telling them that they are wrong.

When we consider using this form of argumentation in groups, we always have some concerns.

"Some kids don't like to talk"

"They will not stay on task."

"One student will do all the talking!"

Try this exercise: At the end of the lesson with five minutes to go, stop teaching. Pretend to be getting something and do not comment about the noise or talk. We guarantee that all the students (or nearly all) will be involved in a conversation. Why? Because they can talk and they are talking about what interests them. Thus, we *can* establish that all kids like to talk and not one of the students was off task in talking to each other. However, what we have to do is orient the conversation so that they are discussing something about what they know.

> **HAVE A GO!**
>
> Argumentation is a key tool in the work of scientists as well as for our students, as we need them as learners to go public with their thinking while negotiating old and new understandings. In Appendix F, explore various ways to get this started in the classroom.

Throughout this chapter we have been talking about big ideas and questioning students during the course of the unit. The intent is for us to engage the students' ideas, to value their thinking, and to assist them to build scientifically acceptable understandings of the concepts. Group work is critical in this process.

Teacher's Voice

Teacher 1: Chris was a boy in second grade who was usually off task and very seldom said anything. One afternoon, during an inquiry on seeds and plants, the students were trying to discover what was inside a lima bean seed. After working in small cooperative groups and making claims and evidence, the children started to share claims and challenge each other. Chris was one of the first ones to disagree with a claim that one of the groups made. At the time, I remember being totally blown away. It was amazing to see Chris so involved in supporting what he believed to be true. As I reflected back on that experience, it made me ever more aware of how important and powerful the language component of the process is. There is real power is seeing kids coming up with a claim, supporting it with evidence, and challenging others when they can't agree.

Teacher 2: My aha moment came when I had one group of students present an argument that changed the way the rest of the class was thinking. They had enough proof to slowly pull all the students to believe in their outcome.

Small-group work is where students can be engaged in laboratory or hands-on activities, debate information shared by the teacher, argue about solutions to problems, frame alternative explanations, and attempt to reach consensus. Small-group work creates opportunities for students who are reluctant to speak in whole-class settings to have their voices heard. As mentioned previously, students are rarely frightened to talk when they are discussing their own ideas. Thus, the activities done in these small groups should be focused on the students exploring their own ideas.

Teacher must take a number of important pedagogical actions with small-group work:

1. Explore different ways to set up the small groups. These range from allowing normal friendship groups to randomly drawing names out of a hat or a purposeful selection by the teacher to assign groups.

2. Make careful decisions about how long you keep the same arrangements of students together. Do not be afraid to change the groups every now and then.

3. As teachers, we need to monitor the conversation occurring in the groups and work out how close the ideas are to the big ideas of the topic. The questions we pose will focus on challenging the students' concepts and how closely they match to the big ideas for the topic.

4. Monitor the time that you have students in small groups. This can be determined when you see that all groups have completed discussions or the activity. This skill gets better with practice. It is important not only to keep the flow of the classroom going but also to allow the students enough time to have meaningful opportunities to engage with what is being asked of them.

5. Remember that when groups are working, your role is to challenge their thinking. When interacting with groups it is important that you do not give answers to the students unless the questions are procedural. We need to have the students understand that you are going to challenge them and that the intent of the exercise is for them to determine the answers.

6. Have mechanisms and strategies in place for all groups to have their ideas or answers in the public view. For example, each group has to put their ideas on the

board or on butcher paper to be hung up. Remember, the intent is for the small group's negotiated position to be further negotiated across the whole class.

There is no one correct way to organize or conduct small groups. As teachers, we have to blend our own styles with various ways to promote opportunities for students to build knowledge. Group work is essential; consequently, we need to explore what particular strategies will be used to set up, monitor, and challenge the groups. It can be very difficult for us as teachers to stop talking, to stop trying to pass on all the knowledge, and to let the students have control of the learning process. Two things are important to remember: (1) Teachers have never had control of the knowledge inside the students' heads, and (2) Small-group work is an ideal, nonthreatening way for all students to be involved in working with their own ideas. Remember, control of the learning process is not control of the learning environment—that is our responsibility as teachers.

The transition between small-group and whole-class discussion is important and can be a challenge as we adjust our pedagogical actions when dealing with these two different situations. Most teachers are comfortable when they engage in discussions with small groups; however, they are uncomfortable when trying to do the same thing in the whole-class setting. The difficult part with the whole-class settings is trying to continue with the concept of challenging students' thinking when you have twenty-five or thirty students rather than four or five in a small group. As a teacher, consider these questions: What strategies are available to examine the small-group outcomes that are different from the traditional teacher-centered, teacher-controlled whole-class discussions? How do you help the whole class come to a consensus about the ideas they have been discussing? How do you make sure that the students' ideas are aligned with the scientifically accepted ideas?

One of the difficult tasks with whole-class work is the need to balance the responsibility we have as teachers to cover the curriculum and where the students are in their understanding. If we can continue to involve the students in a conversation about the concepts, then we can help them make the change. For example, when discussing a particular phenomenon, students will use everyday language. Since we cannot simply tell them what the science word is, we need to enter into negotiation by saying such things as "Instead of using the word X, scientists use the word Y. Is it okay if we use the word Y from now on?" The students generally agree, and then we can begin to use the correct terminology in a manner in which the students can attach meaning to it. Instead of short-term memory games, the students can build conceptual understanding and meaning that will be stored in long-term memory. Another example when working with whole-class settings is to generate some conclusions as a class without referring to any texts. After reaching consensus, ask the students to check the literature to see how what they have come with up matches what the scientists say. If you have managed to steer the questioning and information to the right answer, the students will be comfortable with the answer. If there is a mismatch between their answers and the scientifically acceptable answer, you can immediately instigate a discussion. Again, this discussion will provide opportunities for the students to negotiate their own meaning.

From the Students

As part of their investigation with matter, the students in Ms. Lowell's classroom were asked to make Silly Putty. The students verbally made claims and jotted down their evidence as they interacted with the Silly Putty. The students all wanted the "recipe" so they could go home and make it with their families. Ms. Lowell said, "Well, pull out a piece of paper and write down what you did along with any advice you might have for your family members. Be sure to include your claims and evidence!" Each student began to write. When the students had a draft, Ms. Lowell asked them to share with a small group. Nick and Breanna share their writings in Figures 3.4a and 3.4b. Take note that after hearing Breanna describe how detailed she made her directions, Nick went back and added more detail to the bottom of his original recipe. The negotiation of meaning caught on paper!

Figure 3.4a   *Two third-grade writers negotiate their understanding of what they learned while making Silly Putty elastic dough during a matter unit*

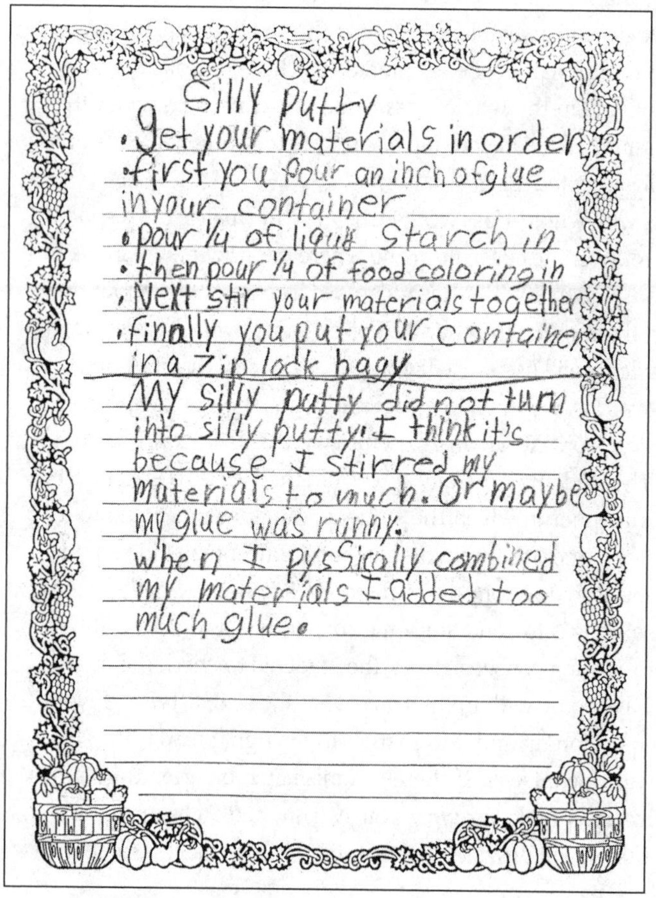

Silly Putty
- get your materials in order
- first you pour an inch of glue in your container
- pour 1/4 of liquid starch in
- then pour 1/4 of food coloring in
- Next stir your materials together
- finally you put your container in a zip lock baggy

My silly putty did not turn into silly putty. I think it's because I stirred my materials to much. Or maybe my glue was runny.

when I pyssically combined my materials I added too much glue.

Figure 3.4b

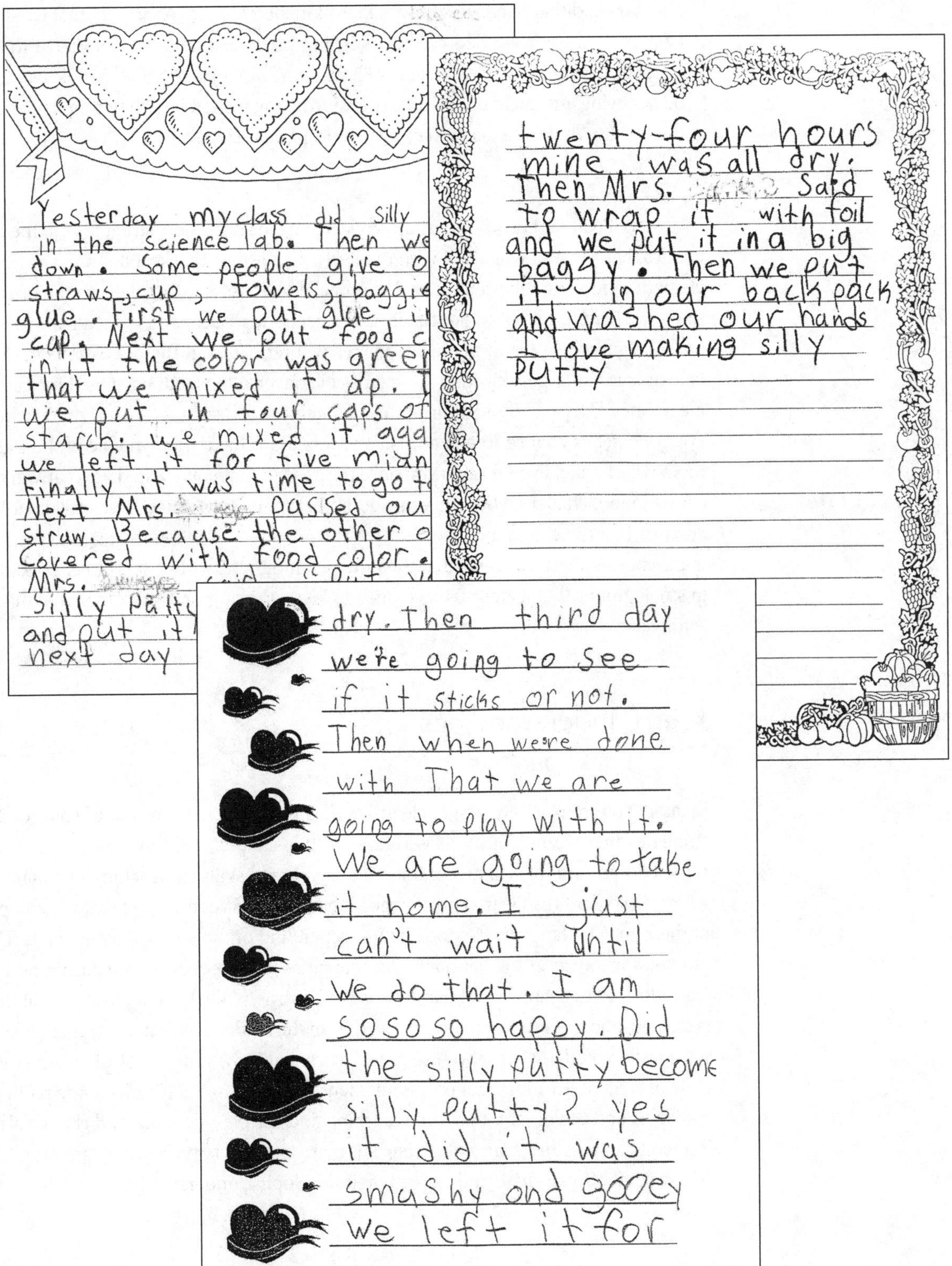

Yesterday my class did silly
in the science lab. Then we
down. Some people give o
straws, cup, towels, baggie
glue. First we put glue i
cup. Next we put food c
in it the color was green
that we mixed it up.
we put in four caps of
starch. we mixed it aga
we left it for five mian
Finally it was time to go t
Next Mrs. _____ passed ou
straw. Because the other o
Covered with food color.
Mrs. _____ said "Put y
Silly Patty
and put it
next day

twenty-four hours
mine was all dry.
Then Mrs. _____ said
to wrap it with foil
and we put it in a big
baggy. Then we put
it in our backpack
and washed our hands
I love making silly
Putty

dry. Then third day
we're going to see
if it sticks or not.
Then when we're done
with That we are
going to play with it.
We are going to take
it home. I just
can't wait Until
we do that. I am
so so so happy. Did
the silly putty become
silly putty? yes
it did it was
smushy and gooey
we left it for

Teacher's Voice

When we were studying the solar system, I asked the students what they felt about NASA. Was it worth the money to explore space? The students had a "discussion" for fifty minutes. They were not shy in sharing their opinions, either! One boy said that of course we should explore outer space. A girl said that would be silly because if we had earthquakes and other disasters here on Earth that needed to be taken care of, instead of having the money to do that, people would be out flying around in outer space. Very intriguing insight into their thinking and their ability to debate using their own conceptual frameworks!

The difficult part of whole-group work is that we as teachers struggle with the dynamics that can and will occur with the lively discussions that result. This is a critical element in moving to inquiry-based approaches. When we struggle with the discussions, we tend to retreat to our traditional didactic approach, and the students seeing the old "guess what is in my head" games will retreat from the discussions. It does take time for us to get skilled at these types of conversations, but never getting started means never trying. By setting up a nonthreatening learning environment where everyone gets a chance to talk and all answers are valued, the dynamic in the classroom will change. Even though you have the answer that you wanted very early in the conversation, challenge the students; do not let them know they have arrived at the answer. Test the confidence they have in the answer. It is when they as a group can make choices about concepts that their understanding will grow. It is easier to do this in small groups, but as teachers we need to keep working on this in the whole-class setting.

Key Understandings

Matching teaching to our views of learning means that we have to change some of the strategies that we use in our classrooms. In this chapter, we have tried to provide some background for what we think are the essential skills for teaching in a manner where all students can learn and engage in the process. We recognize that while some of these may be familiar, they do change depending on how you view learning. The purposes involved in the various skills change as a consequence of focusing on the learning. It does change what happens in the classroom, the type of environment that is created, and the support that is received from the students. We need to change how we question students, how we use group work, and how much control we think we have of student learning. Our encouragement is to keep trying: Work on one particular aspect and the other parts of the teaching and learning dynamic will change also. Remember, *the learner controls learning*. It is up to teachers to orchestrate opportunities where students can share and expand their developing understandings.

CHAPTER 4

Writing as an Essential Element of Science Inquiry

Teacher's Voice

I have gone through some interesting changes as a second-grade teacher while participating in this workshop. First, I have learned the importance of oral language in the learning of young children. The sharing of ideas among the kids during the investigations plays a big part in their learning of new science concepts. The next step really comes from the questions the kids pose during the experiments. Particularly, as a teacher in this process, I've learned to step back and become an active listener. I really listen to the kids now and ask questions accordingly. And you know what? Then they begin to do the same for each other! That response to each other is so important—that generates lots of enthusiasm and excitement, so much so that they can't wait for the next experiment and opportunity to share their learning through talking and writing. Finally, I have learned that the idea as teachers is to adapt not adopt. You have to make the process fit for your age of learners.

In this chapter, we will explore a main underlying philosophical tenet of our work, that is, *without language there is no science*. We know this is a bold statement, but imagine how difficult it would be to teach a science lesson without any form of language—text language, mathematical language, pictorial language, graphical language, or symbolic language. There is no means of doing science, understanding science, or communicating about science without language. Language is *fundamental* to science because we need it to do science and to build further on what we know. To be practicing scientists and *derive* new knowledge, we need language (Norris and Phillips 2003). So we need to recognize that language is important for science and explore how we can incorporate opportunities within our classrooms to allow students to build better understanding of science through engaging with language activities.

In this chapter, we will explore the many ways language—reading, writing, talking, listening, enacting, and visualizing—comes to life in the experience. This exploration will include a critical perspective on current research and practice in relation to science, language, and literacy. In fact, there is much debate currently going on in the research field about how best to use writing within our classrooms. The two major views are opposites of each other: learning how to use language and using language to learn. Each view is explored in the following sections.

Learning How to Use Language

Many researchers have suggested that to be successful in science, students must learn the language patterns of science before they engage in the practices of scientists. In some cases, with this thinking, the act of reading and writing in science are taught as skills that must be learned before students engage in the act of science inquiry. Examples of this thinking follow:

1. Students must learn to practice writing up a laboratory report as a critical function of science. They need to know what the laboratory report structure is and how scientists use it.

2. We need to ensure that students have the correct vocabulary prior to engaging in the topic so that they can recognize the terms in the textbook that they have. This word list should be given to students prior to the unit.

3. We need to teach students about the structure of argument separate from inquiry so that they can argue about topics.

These examples illustrate a position that students need to learn the mechanics of the language. We refer to this position as a mechanistic position. While there have been a number of studies conducted to determine the value of this particular position, the results are inconclusive (Klein 1999).

Using Language to Learn

The opposite position to the previous one is that students learn through using the language; that is, the language is introduced to them as a process of being involved in the science lessons. Language practices become embedded within the science lessons as a means to help students construct understanding. Examples of this follow:

1. Having completed an experiment activity, students explore the structure of a report to present their findings and conclusions to the teacher and the class.

2. Students are introduced to science terminology when there is a need for the term so that they can build connections to their meaning.

3. Students are introduced to scientific argumentation as a consequence of having to discuss, debate, and defend their results and conclusions.

We refer to this position as the language-to-learn position. Here, students can learn *about* the language as a process of *using* the language. While there have not been many studies that have explored this position in science classrooms, the results to date have been positive in terms of helping students learn science (Klein 1999).

From the Students

In Figure 4.1, a kindergarten student shares her developing understanding during a science unit on push-pull. This is an example of an embedded language practice; the student has just completed an investigation with dominoes and writes her developing understanding in her science notebook. It says: "I think that those dominoes could surround those other dominoes and then the dominoes can knock down other ones."

Figure 4.1 *Kindergarten student writing a claim about her work with dominoes*

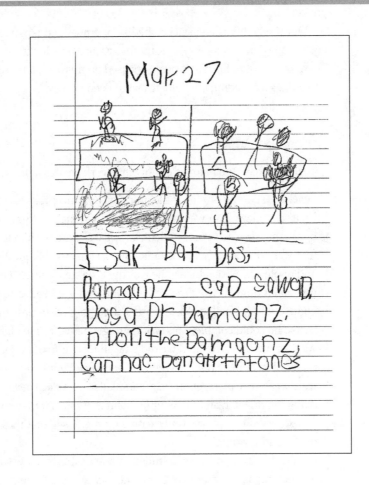

Which Position on Language Should We Use?

We believe that to enhance student learning, teachers should use language as a learning tool. Building on the work of theorists such as Gee (1996) and Lemke (1990), we believe that students will have greater connections to science and the language of science if they can build from what they know. Students need to have a purpose to engage in the language practices of scientists—simply to have to use language because it is important for the topic is not motivating enough for students. We need to create reasons for students to have to engage in using the language of science. Students are voting with their feet; they do not go on to science careers because they cannot connect to science. They do not see purposes for engaging with science.

The language-to-learn movement is more aligned with learning as described in Chapter 2 than is the mechanistic view of learning language. If we allow students to use what they know as the beginning point of using language, then we engage with what they know, not what is external to them. If the understanding of the science and the language is built within the context of science through embedded language practices, then student confidence in both the science *and* language becomes much greater.

Our research has focused on the use of embedded language practices within science inquiry in elementary classrooms, particularly focusing on the act of writing. Therefore, most of the discussion is focused on this area, although we do weave in opportunities for reading and talking as the need arises.

Teacher's Voice

Teachers share their stories of how this work creates a purpose for writing:

Teacher 1: During our life-cycle unit, for the conceptual questions on the pretest, I had a student who was struggling with writing anything down for one of the questions. He was a good student, so this was hard for him to deal with. After our unit was completed, when it came time to answer the questions again, he wrote and wrote and wrote. In fact, he was the last one writing. When I asked him if he was about done, he told me he had a lot more he needed to write. He ended up going out in the hall to finish, being willing to give up class time for another subject so he could complete his writing to get across to me all that he had learned! Also for our life-cycle unit, we did a tie-in for our final project with a benchmark for English: doing a research report. Then, using nonfiction material, the students were to write a short report on an animal's life cycle. They were so excited about doing the research and the writing that many asked if they could do more reports for extra credit. That was very exciting for me to see that they wanted to do more reading and writing!

Teacher 2: On his own, a student made a table to show some observations he was getting during our plant tests. The idea spread! Others started making similar graphs in their science notebooks. The students carried this on over the course of the unit. They included lots of important information.

Teacher 3: One group was certain that their claim was "right" and the other five groups' claims were "not right"! After intense negotiation the five other groups convinced the first group that their claim had some serious flaws. This group decided that they needed to change their claim and evidence in order to demonstrate the change in their thinking. They created charts and posters to demonstrate this new thinking to others in the class. What a powerful use of writing to demonstrate thinking!

What Is Happening When Students Are Writing?

A number of different theories are used to try to explain how we learn by writing about a topic. These theories do recognize that simply asking students to recall information is not a writing-to-learn experience. That is, asking students to list the parts of a flower or to write down the first twenty elements of the periodic table are simply recall tasks and are not viewed as learning tasks. However, when writing is viewed as a learning task, the differences between the theories essentially revolve around the idea that when someone undertakes a writing task in science, they use two knowledge bases— the science-content knowledge base and the language knowledge base.

In classrooms, then, we must structure opportunities for students to engage in writing that will allow them to "ideate." Ideating (Goodman 2003) is the act of bringing both of these knowledge bases together to negotiate meaning, in this case, on paper. One way teachers in elementary classrooms have created this *space* for students to write to learn is through science notebooks. These notebooks should be more than just a history of observations made. They are an ongoing thinking space, where students are ideating about questions, claims, evidence, what others say, and reflective statements about how their thinking has changed.

Teacher's Voice

Teachers share their strategies for using science notebooks in elementary classrooms:

Teacher 1: Science journals in my classroom are used to plan experiments and write down personal ideas. I also like to see my students compare the thoughts of their classmates and group members. Students are able to reflect in their journals about lessons and units.

Teacher 2: At the beginning of the year, the students decorate the front of their notebooks so that they reflect the students' interests in science. Most kids cut out pictures and words from magazines to personalize their cover. We also divide the notebook into sections, for example, *Buzzwords* (vocabulary), *Information from others*, *Inquiry*, and *Reflection*. We made tabs to label each section. We also spent time discussing how scientists use notebooks and how the students would use their notebooks to record their investigations and learning throughout the year. All of this gave the students ownership and helped keep their notebooks organized.

When we consider the audience for the act of ideating, we should not diminish the importance of writing for oneself at times. Writing for oneself is a way to ideate or to wonder and explore your own belief, thoughts, and developing understandings. Additionally, there are multiple ways to demonstrate this negotiation of meaning: sketching, diagramming, writing down intriguing statements or ideas, making lists. All this occurs in a safe place where children can mess around with their developing ideas. Exploring their own thinking processes highlights students' awareness of their own learning capabilities. This is typically not a form of writing that is graded.

From the Students

In this third-grade classroom, notebooks began the year organized in a simple spiral notebook and soon became "messy" (as described by the students). They taped in data charts and newspaper articles. Sticky notes with questions and the names of good books that helped in answering researchable questions were also found protruding out of notebooks, to mark particular spots that the young scientist needed to return to at a later date. In this particular example, a student wrote down the characteristics of different forms of matter to inform his claim about how gas, liquids, and solids change. This teacher tries to balance how much she controls the notebook. Her hope is that 50 percent is student driven and the teacher and other members of the classroom influence the other 50 percent.

Figure 4.2   *An example from a third-grade student's notebook during a matter unit*

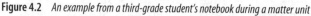

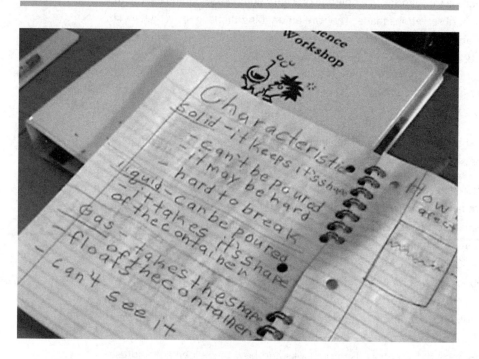

Writing as ideating is just one aspect of writing that is essential to the approach (Goodman 2003). Writing-to-learn strategies also weave throughout the experience as students write for purpose; in other words, there is a reason to write because students need to write to think, to record observations, to make claims, to gather evidence, and to communicate with various audiences.

CHECK THE EXPERTS

We have found many resources useful as we have considered how to use writing-to-learn strategies in our elementary classrooms. Two particular resources that we have found helpful follow:

Science Notebooks: Writing About Inquiry by Lori Fulton and Brian Campbell (Heinemann, 2003).

The Science Workshop: Reading, Writing and Thinking Like a Scientist by Wendy Saul, Jeanne Reardon, Charles R. Pearce, Donna Dieckman, and Donna Neutze (Heinemann, 2002).

During one school-year workshop, the teachers decided to read these two texts as part of a professional book club. The teachers who read about notebooks presented their thinking in the form of questions, which stimulated grand conversations and encouraged our own form of argumentation as we attempted to negotiate a new understanding about the teaching and learning benefits (and drawbacks) to using this notebook idea. The key questions and considerations discussed by the group follow:

What type of notebook will you use?

What information will you expect the students to include in all entries?

What are realistic expectations for your students' writing?

What organizational tools will your students need?

How will you assess the notebooks?

What do you expect/hope to accomplish with notebooks?

How will your expectations change over time?

Who will control what goes in the notebook?

How and when will you provide time to reflect?

What evidence of conceptual understanding will you look for in the notebooks?

What opportunities can you provide for students to connect their notebooks to reading?

Students in classrooms also write to record thinking and results. We will explore the template in Chapter 5, but one of the essential functions of the language is the *heuristic* function of the language, meaning using language to think, to question, to wonder.

Figure 4.3a *Kindergarten example of writing to learn*

Figure 4.3b *Second-grade example of writing to learn*

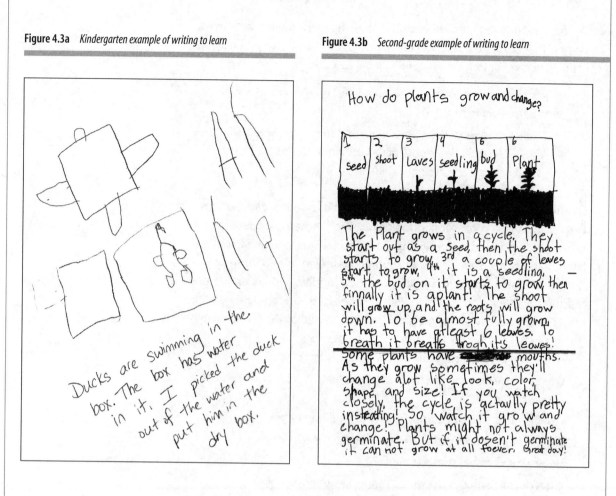

Another essential component to writing in the classroom is the summary-writing experience. At the conclusion of each unit, students are asked to compose a summary of their learning, often in unique forms and for different audiences. This task is not simply a report or presentation of learning; it is in the act of creating this summary that students continue to learn as they negotiate what they have learned and how they currently understand the topic within their own individual conceptual frameworks. More information about the summary-writing experience will be explored in Chapter 8.

From the Students

This poster was created as part of a summary-writing experience during a plant unit in a fifth-grade classroom. Note how the student uses common text features to organize her poster. In order for students to write to learn, student must read. Using non-fiction books as well as science textbooks provides students with an opportunity to familiarize themselves with the style and language of writers, so that they too can belong to the community of writers.

Figure 4.4   *Kiwi poster demonstrating learning about plants, created by a fifth-grade student*

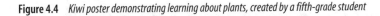

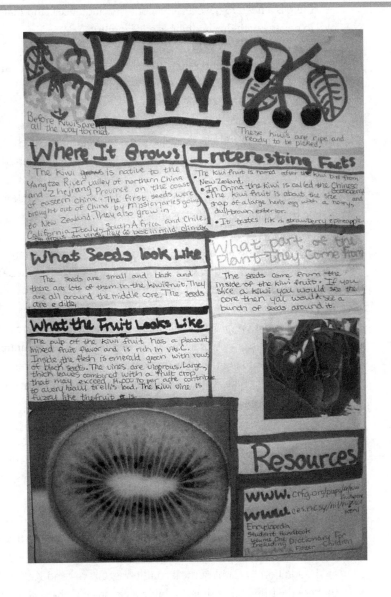

Essential Elements Needed to Write

Over the past fifty years, a great deal of research has focused on the act of writing (Bazerman 2008). It is important for our work in classrooms to consider the research and theory that have indicated the essential elements needed to support our students as developing writers. It was Brian Cambourne (1987) who listed the seven conditions for literacy learning. Each condition has an important role in the classroom:

1. Immersion. Students must be immersed in various opportunities to use language within science—reading, writing, talking, and listening. This immersion means there is a need to have a variety of texts, audiences, and materials for our students to engage with during their science inquiry.

2. Demonstration. Rather than modeling and expecting our students to do exactly as we do, ongoing demonstrations of using language are necessary for the students to learn how to use language.

3. Expectation. Teachers must have the expectation that children can and will use language given the opportunity. This applies to *all* students.

4. Responsibility. When given the opportunity and expectation, then students must be trusted and given the responsibility to use language.

5. Use. If students are expected to sit quietly and never use language or are never able to pick up the pen themselves, they will never use the language and thus will have difficulty learning the language.

6. Approximation. Yes, we must make mistakes when we are learning to use the language. Many of us will say we have learned more from our mistakes than from our successes! In language, this may mean that students will use invented spellings when appropriate, and in science, it may mean that we need to give students time to question their misconceptions.

7. Response. A key condition is that all writers need response—response from their peers, from their teachers, from family, and from other members of their audience. This feedback is essential in continued development as a writer.

Finally, Cambourne states that this is all a moot point if there is no *engagement*. Also, for students to engage, they must feel comfortable in taking the risk with their thinking and developing understandings.

In addition to Cambourne's conditions, Graves and Kittle (2005) also remind us that good writing takes time. To build a classroom where children can write to learn, time and space must be given for writers to engage in their work. Also, Graves men-

From the Students

This page from a third-grade student's book illustrates her understandings about sound. Here the student uses text and pictures to display her thinking and developing conceptual frameworks on the topic.

Figure 4.5 *Third-grade student's developing understanding about sound*

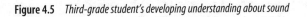

tions choice as a key to motivating writers. Choice in materials, topic, form, and audience are all possible ways to weave choice into an experience. Finally, we also know writers need time for reflecting—time to think about the elements of good writing as well as time to read from good authors and to examine their own strengths and weaknesses as a reader and writer.

From the Students

In this example, a sixth-grade student transfers her learning about cells to a diary entry about how this all can be tied to the stuffed animals in her room at home.

Figure 4.6 *Student diary entry about cells*

Dear Diary,

Today I learned about the Animal Eukaryotic cell. I wonder what stuff animals in my room would be which organelle in the cell. I would probably chose my stuffed lion for the nucleus, because the nucleus directs the activity of the cell. The lion could tell everyone what to do. Since the lion is the king of the jungle. For the E.R. I would chose a stuffed snake because its cury and could tranfer protein (ribosomes) throughout the cell. The Kangaroo would be the lysosomes because it could store the cells waste in its pooch. I would chose my stuffed crab, Crabby, for mitochondria because he could break down food in its claws and release energy through its legs. I would chose a my stuffed dog, Roxy, to have the job of the golgi bodies she could fetch the protein inside the cell and give it to the outside of the cell. I would chose a fish for the cytoplasm because its kind of jelly and could hold the cell water and nutrients. For the cell membrane I would chose a bear because it could let certain things in and out by telling them if they can come in or not. For the nuclear member I would chose my bee, honey, because if the nucleus got to close to the cytoplasm she could sting him to let him move over. The cells vaculole would be a stork because it could store the materials for the cell in its big mouth. Write more later.

In addition, when we consider how to support all learners in our classroom, a balanced literacy curriculum should call for the gradual release of responsibility, that we present a variety of opportunities for our students, including a natural balance between teacher and student control of the writing. For example, in a kindergarten classroom, the teacher may have experiences where she holds the pen and the students as a group dictate to her their thinking—this is called a shared writing experience. In an older elementary classroom, this may happen when children construct a text together with the teacher as she writes on an overhead projector. This is teacher-controlled

The connection between reading and writing has been well researched over the past thirty years. Stotsky (1983) published a review of correlational and experimental research studies that examined the influence of reading and writing relationships. Her synthesis spans about fifty years, from the beginning of the 1930s to 1981. Studies showed that better readers tended to be better writers, that better writers read more than poor writers, and that better readers produce more syntactically mature writing than poor readers. From the research studies, correlation studies presented consistent results of a significant correlation between reading and writing.

In addition, Tierney et al. (1989) conducted a study on the effects of reading and writing upon thinking critically. The study examined the effects of writing, reading, and answering questions, both separately and in combination with one another. This study questioned whether writing in combination with reading prompts more critical thinking than reading or writing done separately, or in combination with questions or a knowledge-activation activity. The study examined the amount and type of reading that learners engage in as they read, as they write, or as they both read and write. The study revealed that the students who read and wrote were engaged in a great deal more evaluative thinking and perspective shifting than those who just wrote or those who just read. Also, reading and writing in combination contributed to a wide range of revisions and to a higher quality of drafts than writing alone. The study presented a view of reading and writing working together for goals, which transcend either reading or writing for their own ends. Furthermore, the study supported the view that reading and writing in combination have the potential to contribute to powerful ways to thinking.

writing. On the other end, we would find student-controlled writing where students are in control of the pen and what they will write about. In the middle of this spectrum are all forms of writing including guided writing (where the teacher may give the students a sentence starter or a frame for writing) and partner writing (where the teacher no longer controls the pen but neither does the individual student; he or she must now negotiate with a peer or multiple peers). None of these strategies or methods is wrong; however, the idea is to balance who has the power of the pen, and it is when the classroom is truly student centered that we can create the best learning environment for students.

All writers need opportunities to write, read, and discuss their writing. Children's books and other texts can provide powerful models and demonstrations for our students that can help them consider genre, theme, style, audience, and other text features. We encourage our students to learn from authors of both fiction and nonfiction to inform their own writing.

From the Students

In this example, kindergarten students were given the unique task of taking home a disposable camera and looking for certain objects to explore properties. In Figures 4.7a and 4.7b is one student's checklist of pictures she was supposed to take. In the photo on the right, the student displays her "frame" book. Here the student placed the picture she took with a frame sentence, "Someone reading is _____." Then the students put the appropriate word to match their picture on the line. This became a fabulous compare-and-contrast activity as students would open their books all to the same page and see what everyone had for something LOUD or something you can SMELL.

Figures 4.7a and 4.7b *A kindergarten student shares her work*

Picture List

Take a picture of . . .

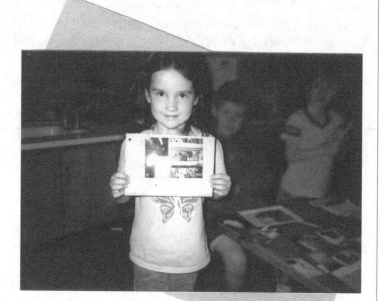

- ☐ Someone reading
  mom reading to Emma
- ☐ Something alive
  my cat Trixie
- ☐ Something in a container
  my little ponys
- ☐ Someone writing
  mom writing
- ☐ Something cold
  Dairy Queen visit
- ☐ Someone having fun
  my sister Emma dressed up
- ☐ Something tall
  bunk beds
- ☐ Your favorite thing
  class picture of my friends
- ☐ Something red
  my dad's truck
- ☐ Something that doesn't move
  our house
- ☐ Someone doing math
  mom doing math
- ☐ Something loud
  my alarm clock
- ☐ Something you can smell
  an orange
- ☐ Something old
  our camper
- ☐ Something you plug in
  our TV

Teacher's Voice

We are often asked the question: "What about young children who can verbally articulate but can't get that thinking into writing?" Teachers respond:

Response #1: You start off with an experiment. The student could draw and label different stages of what was happening and verbally explain to the teacher or peers, or use a tape recorder or videotape. Another idea is to purposefully group or pair students together so that each group contains a child who has good control of the writing process, so that together the group can discuss and share their findings, and this could move into the writing.

Response #2: A student who can't do his own writing can draw his thoughts. In a cooperative group all contribute ideas and one is the recorder. A peer can do the writing or the teacher can write while the student dictates. The teacher can record everyone's ideas on the board.

Response #3: Model whole group for them—they talk and I am the recorder. Draw pictures and label them, if they can. Provide part of the sentence for them. Prepare writing material for them that they can illustrate, or find clip art that they can add their experiments.

Key Considerations in Using Language in the Science Classroom

In closing, we need to revisit three key components to writing in the science classroom: purpose, function, and audience. These considerations are what make the difference for student learning in relation to language and science. First, language use and science inquiry need to have a clear purpose. With no reason to use the language, our efforts will be futile—students will see no purpose in its use, and we will have little hope of creating a space where the students will question their own conceptual frameworks. This purpose is closely tied to the function of the language and the presence of a true audience.

Also, in considering the function of the language, we must remember to create opportunities to engage in language in different ways using a variety of forms. In classrooms, students learn to persuade, to inform, to question, to wonder, to regulate, to imagine, to collaborate, and to argue. In using these embedded language practices, students are experiencing and learning about the various functions of the language through their use. Oftentimes, minilessons present themselves as an opportunity to explore certain aspects of the language. We call this just-in-time instruction because it grows from what the students need in relation to language use just at the time they need it—while engaging in science inquiry.

Does this mean we never teach skills about writing? Of course we do. In her popular book, *The Art of Teaching Writing*, Lucy Calkins encouraged teachers in one entire chapter, titled "Don't be afraid to teach" (1994, p. 193). In this chapter, she introduces the ideas of minilessons, or—the term we like to use—just-in-time instruction. That is, we pay attention to what our students are learning and struggling with and swoop in "just in time" to provide support and needed information. In Figure 4.9, an overhead

From the Students

A third-grade student had an important purpose for writing during a milk experiment as part of a matter unit. He placed his question and observations right on the brown paper towel under this milk container!

Figure 4.8 *A third-grade milk experiment—thinking in action*

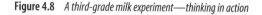

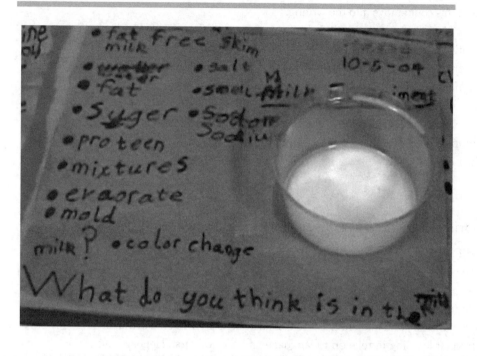

remains as an artifact of this third-grade teacher's just-in-time instruction. She noticed that in her students' writing, they were failing to link their ideas about matter together while writing a paragraph about their most recent investigation. Realizing many students were struggling with this, she stepped to the projector and started drawing and explaining how to link ideas together like a train. Her students are from a small rural town where the majority of the population is linked to the many railroad companies that converge and have offices in the community. When she helped the students understand that writing a paragraph is like linking up a train, it made sense to the students. The engine has to be strong and signal what is to come, like a topic sentence. Then, each of the cars to come must hook to the next or the paragraph derails. At the end is a caboose, or a beaming strobe light, which signals to the next train where it is. The final sentence of the paragraph needs to signal the main ideas, or the big idea, to leave the audience knowing where you are—make a claim. This group of third-grade students revisited this lesson again and again. Just-in-time instruction—when the students need it with purpose. Don't be afraid to teach.

From the Students

In this overhead example, a third-grade teacher demonstrates how to write a paragraph during a minilesson while studying matter.

Figure 4.9 *A writing minilesson on constructing a paragraph*

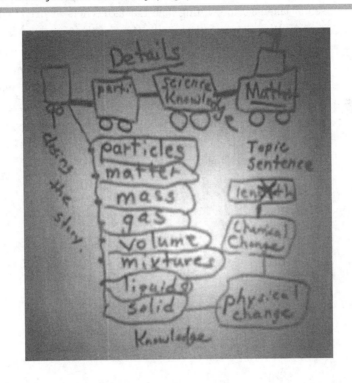

Finally, the importance of students having a true audience for their writing cannot be understated. This audience can be known or unknown, nearby or faraway. Students can write to peers, family members, penpals, other classrooms, and the like. Ideally, it is important that the audience is able to give some form of feedback to the writer, either written or oral. This feedback offers one more opportunity to the learner to negotiate meaning. Not only do students need this feedback at the end, they need this opportunity for ongoing discussion throughout the inquiry process and any time they write. It always fuels the writing process to talk with a partner or a small group.

Throughout the next section (Chapters 5 through 8), we expand on many of the ideas presented in this chapter and give many more classroom examples of how this work comes to life in the elementary grades, including a discussion about assessing student learning in Chapter 8.

We conclude with the wise words of a second-grade student who reminds us of what is important about language use and writing, "Ya know, when I write, I think, and when I think, then I have to write more, and if I write more, then I think more and wow, my brain is just going to keep growing and growing—it just goes round and round: write, think, write, think, think, write!"

Key Understandings

In this chapter, we have tried to provide some background of what we think are the essential language and writing skills that as teachers we need to use when using the approach. We recognize that while some of these may be familiar, they do change depending on how we view learning and how we organize writing tasks in the classroom. The purposes involved in the various writing skills change as a consequence of focusing on the learning and with consideration to topic, type, purpose, audience, and the method of text production. Assessing this writing is also an important consideration, but with a reminder of who controls learning, it is essential to include the student in this assessment process by allowing the audience for the writing to provide key feedback and assessment in addition to the teacher.

Creating a Space in the Classroom for Questions, Claims, and Evidence

Figure II.1 *Preschool student gathering evidence for a unit on "Animals have basic needs"*

During a recent open house, a fourth-grade student was sharing with her mother what she had been learning in science. Her mother looked at the top of the paper and said, "What does SWH stand for?"

Without missing a beat, she looked at her mother and says, "S—W—H: See—What—Happens!"

This fourth-grade student's insight has become one of our favorite language stories. *SWH* actually stands for the Science Writing Heuristic approach to teaching and learning in science. We often get into "trouble" with this title because many believe the term *heuristic* is too difficult for people to access, and it often just turns them away without asking more questions to understand what it means for teaching and learning. So then, what is meant by heuristic? In language circles, we use the term to talk about the ability to use language to question, to wonder, or to investigate. Imagine if the photograph in Figure II.1 were to suddenly begin like a movie. Would we hear this child engaging in the heuristic function of our language by wondering out loud about the chicks and ducks in the box? Would he pose a question? Would he have a claim about animals and their basic needs? In cognitive theory, a heuristic is a template for thinking. Take a moment to look it up in the dictionary—there are many other interesting uses of the word. In the following paragraphs, we will describe the SWH approach.

The SWH approach is embedded in the knowledge base that was presented in the previous section. It is based on the foundation that only the learner controls learning, and it is the teacher's challenge to orchestrate opportunities for students to engage as learners. With this in mind, Carolyn Keys and Brian Hand in 1997 developed the Science Writing Heuristic (SWH) as an approach to use in school classrooms and, with this dual purpose in mind, created two plans: one for learners, and the second, for teachers (see Figure II.2). This approach has been investigated extensively over the past ten years in early childhood, elementary, middle school, high school, and college classrooms (see Chapter 10 for a list of articles related to this research).

The SWH approach consists of a framework to guide activities as well as a metacognitive support, or support of thinking about thinking, to prompt student reasoning about data. Similar to Gowin's Vee heuristic (1981, p. 157), the SWH approach provides learners with a heuristic template to guide science activity and reasoning in writing and provides teachers with a template of suggested strategies to enhance learning from science inquiry activities. As a whole, the activities and thinking provide authentic meaning-making opportunities for learners. The negotiation of meaning occurs across multiple formats for discussion, reading, and writing. The SWH approach is designed as a bridge between informal, expressive writing modes that foster personally constructed science understandings and more formal, public modes that focus on traditional forms of reasoning in science. In this way the heuristic scaffolds learners in both understanding their own science inquiry activity and connecting this knowledge to other science ideas. The template for student thinking prompts learners to generate questions, claims, and evidence. It also prompts them to compare their findings with others, including their peers and information from nonfiction literature, the Internet, or other sources. The template for student thinking also prompts learners to reflect on how their own ideas have changed during the experience of the science inquiry activity. The SWH approach can be understood as an alternative format for laboratory reports. Instead of responding to the five traditional sections—purpose, methods, observations, results, and conclusions—students are expected to respond to prompts eliciting questioning, knowledge claims, evidence, description of data and observations, and meth-

The Science Writing Heuristic, Part I

A plan for teacher-designed activities to promote laboratory understanding

1. Exploration of pre-instruction understanding through individual or group concept mapping

2. Pre-laboratory activities, including informal writing, making observations, brainstorming, and posing questions

3. Participation in laboratory activity

4. Negotiation phase I—writing personal meanings for laboratory activity (for example, writing journals)

5. Negotiation phase II—sharing and comparing data interpretations in small groups (for example, making group charts)

6. Negotiation phase III—comparing science ideas to textbooks for other printed resources (for example, writing group notes in response to focus questions)

7. Negotiation phase IV—individual reflection and writing (for example, creating a presentation such as a poster or report for a larger audience)

8. Exploration of post-instruction understanding through concept mapping

The Science Writing Heuristic, Part II

A plan for students

1. Beginning ideas—What are my questions?

2. Tests—What did I do?

3. Observations—What did I see?

4. Claims—What can I claim?

5. Evidence—How do I know? Why am I making these claims?

6. Reading—How do my ideas compare with others' ideas?

7. Reflection—How have my ideas changed?

Figure II.2
The two plans for the SWH approach: The teacher plan and the student plan

ods, and to reflect on changes to their own thinking. We will discuss how to get this started by asking good questions in Chapter 5.

While the SWH approach recognizes the need for students to conduct laboratory investigations that develop their understanding of scientific methods and procedures, the teachers' template also seeks to provide a stronger pedagogical focus for this learning. In other words, the SWH approach is based on the assumption that science writing tasks in school should reflect some of the characteristics of scientists' writing but should also be shaped as teaching tools to encourage students to "unpack" scientific meaning and reasoning. The SWH approach is intended to promote both scientific thinking and reasoning in the inquiry experience, as well as metacognition, where learners become aware of the basis of their knowledge and are able to monitor their learning more explicitly. Because the SWH approach focuses on traditional forms of scientific thinking, such as the development of links between claims and evidence, it also has the potential to build learners' understandings of the nature of science, strengthen conceptual understandings, and engage them in the authentic argumentation process of science. The making of claims and providing supporting evidence will be explored in Chapter 6.

The SWH approach emphasizes the collaborative nature of scientific activity, that is, scientific argumentation, where learners are expected to engage in a continuous cycle of negotiating and clarifying meanings and explanations with their peers and teacher. In other words, the SWH approach is designed to promote classroom discussion where students' personal explanations and observations are tested against the perceptions and contributions of the broader group. Learners are encouraged to make explicit and defensible connections between questions, observations, data, claims, and evidence. When students state a claim for an investigation, they are expected to describe a pattern, make a generalization, state a relationship, or construct an explanation. We will discuss this more in Chapter 7.

The SWH approach promotes students' participation in setting their own investigative agenda for laboratory work, framing questions, proposing methods to address these questions, and carrying out appropriate investigations. Such an approach to laboratory work is advocated in many national science curriculum documents on the grounds that this freedom of choice will promote greater student engagement and motivation with topics. However, in practice much laboratory work follows a narrow teacher agenda that does not allow for broader questioning or more diverse data interpretation. When procedures are uniform for all students, where data are similar, and where claims match expected outcomes, then the reporting of results and conclusions often seems meaningless to students and lacks opportunities for deeper student learning about the topic or for developing scientific reasoning skills. To address these issues the SWH is designed to provide scaffolding for purposeful thinking about the relationships between questions, evidence, and claims. A discussion about the summary-writing experience and reflection can be found in Chapter 8.

In the following four chapters, we will take you through the SWH approach step by step, continually returning to the lessons we learned in the first four chapters about teaching, learning, and writing. As our insightful fourth-grade student would say, "See What Happens!"

CHAPTER 5

What Makes a Question Good?

You know what makes a question really good? When it makes
your head hurt! You know what I mean? Like, you can ask me
an easy question, like what color is that grass . . . that doesn't
make my brain have to work at all. It just falls out of my
mouth—no thinking. But ask me a really good question . . .
like, where does the sun go at night? Yeah, that question is
going to put my brain to work.
—*Comment from a third-grade student*

The natural world provides mysteries and wonders that can perplex and cause all of us to think: "I wonder . . ." "Why?" "What would happen if . . . ?" We are constantly negotiating our understanding of the world around us.
Children are inquisitive by nature. From the time children begin to talk they have many questions. The number of questions children ask often amazes parents with toddlers and preschoolers. When our children were young, it seemed as if we spent all day answering questions like: "Why is the sky blue?" "Why is the sun so bright?" "Why is the grass green?" As soon as we answered one question, another would immediately follow. Some days it seems as though all we do is answer questions!

In the classroom, preschool and kindergarten teachers find themselves continually answering questions posed by students. At this age children want to investigate and are curious about many different things. We encourage this curiosity about the world by providing many active learning opportunities, including time to play, work in groups, and talk to their peers, as well as provide time for them to look in books and draw pictures. Most important, we read many, many books to them.

However, by the time students are in sixth grade, we notice something different about them. They appear to be less willing to ask questions. What happened to all the questions these students had when they younger? Talking to teachers and observing in classrooms we have noticed that this reluctance to ask questions seems to be happening earlier in students' school lives as teachers try to cover more and more material at a younger age and students have fewer opportunities to be actively engaged.

As teachers then, if we want our students to ask questions and think about the world around them, we have to provide an environment that promotes the curiosity that intuitively we know still exists in our students. The same types of opportunities we provide for younger students need to be incorporated into all classrooms to encourage curiosity and engage students in critical thinking and questioning. If students are to be in charge of negotiating meaning and understanding, they need to have opportunities to discuss, read, write, think, and explore.

To encourage questions for inquiry in our classrooms we need to have in place an environment that supports questioning and critical thinking. Thinking critically involves risk on the part of the student. Jerry Thacker (1991) suggested that educators should engage in the following teacher behaviors to support students in critical thinking:

- ❖ Set ground rules well in advance
- ❖ Provide well-planned activities
- ❖ Show respect for each student
- ❖ Promote nonthreatening activities
- ❖ Be flexible
- ❖ Accept individual differences
- ❖ Exhibit positive attitudes
- ❖ Model thinking skills
- ❖ Acknowledge every response
- ❖ Allow students to be active participants
- ❖ Create experiences that will ensure success at least part of the time for every student
- ❖ Use a wide variety of teacher modalities

In this chapter, we will discuss ways to encourage and support the natural curiosity of students through the SWH process. Since questioning is the focus of this chapter, the questions we will discuss follow:

- ❖ What makes a question good?
- ❖ What kinds of questions do we need to ask to help students negotiate meaning?
- ❖ Where do we get questions to investigate?
- ❖ How do we get started?
- ❖ How do we help students ask questions that are worth investigating? In other words, how do we help them move beyond the yes/no, fact-based questions?
- ❖ What's the difference between researchable and testable questions?

What Makes a Question Good?

In order to answer this question it is helpful to think about our own understanding of critical thinking and questioning. Research by Friedman and Lee (1996) and others tell us that there is a strong relationship between teacher questions and student response. Higher-level questioning leads to better student achievement and better understanding.

CHECK THE EXPERTS

Bloom's Taxonomy is a framework for critical thinking. As you may recall, Bloom's Taxonomy identifies six levels of thinking ranging from Level I—Knowledge to Level VI—Evaluation. Categories are not absolute and may overlap, but they are fairly easy to understand. Related to this taxonomy is a tool that is useful in thinking of how to develop good questions as a teacher and help students develop an understanding of good questions for investigation. Developed in consultation with the work of Fowler (1996), this question-stem generator helps teachers to think about how to ask questions of students that make them think deeply about science. Here is a summary of each level with sample questions:

❖ Level I—Knowledge: Students exhibit memory of previous learned materials, terms, basic concepts, and answers. Examples of questions at the knowledge level include:

  • What is . . . ?
  • Can you recall . . . ?
  • Which one?
  • Can you list the three . . . ?

❖ Level II—Comprehension. Students demonstrate understanding of facts and ideas of organizing, translating, interpreting, giving descriptions, and stating main ideas. Examples of questions at the comprehension level include:

  • How would you compare . . . ? Contrast?
  • What facts or ideas show . . . ?
  • What statements support . . . ?

❖ Level III—Application: Students solve problems to new situations by applying acquired knowledge, facts, techniques, and rules in a different way. Examples of questions at the application level include:

  • What examples can you find to . . . ?
  • What other way would you plan to . . . ?
  • How would you apply what you learned to develop . . . ?

❖ Level IV—Analysis: Students examine and break information into parts by identifying motives or causes and finding evidence to support generalizations. Sample questions at this level:

  • How is . . . related to . . . ?
  • Why do you think . . . ?
  • What conclusions can you draw?

❖ Level V—Synthesis: Synthesis involves compiling information in a different way by combining elements in a new pattern or proposing alternative solutions.

  • How would you test . . . ?
  • Can you predict the outcome if . . . ?
  • What would happen if . . . ?

❖ Level VI—Evaluation: Evaluation involves presenting and defending opinions by making judgments about information, the validity of ideas, or the quality of work based on a set of criteria.

  • What data was used to make the conclusion?
  • How would you determine . . . ?

What Kinds of Questions Do We Need to Ask to Help Students Negotiate Meaning?

Facts and an understanding of how to comprehend those facts are important to help us understand the big picture or concept. But if we ask only factual questions, we get only fact-based, knowledge-level answers. Using the questions related to Bloom's Taxonomy helped us to move our questions beyond the fact and knowledge level to those questions that lead to deeper thinking, synthesis, and evaluation. Students are in charge of their learning, but the questions we ask of them can help them to negotiate their meaning by spurring them to think more deeply about a topic. So, to help students negotiate meaning, we have to be mindful of the types of questions we ask.

HAVE A GO!

Time to have a go with questioning. Explore how to ask good questions in Appendix D.

Understanding how to ask and use higher-level thinking questions is very important as discussions begin and grow in your classroom around the big idea. When students are working individually or in small groups, the questions should be designed to promote deeper thinking to help negotiate their understanding of that big idea.

Thinking about answers to questions takes time. Students need time to process the questions and think about their answers. Research from the Northwest Regional Educational Laboratory (2001) on questioning shows that asking higher-order questions during classroom discussions and lengthening wait time during classroom questioning are two ways to promote the development of thinking skills. Typical teacher wait time is less than one second before asking another question, calling on another student, or providing an answer themselves. When asking higher-level thinking questions, a minimum of three seconds is necessary. This research found that increasing teacher wait time beyond three seconds leads to improvement in student achievement as well as the length of student responses. It may take as much as thirty to forty-five seconds or longer for some struggling learners to process information and respond. This wait time feels like an eternity in the classroom. Asking good questions, questions at a higher level to promote thinking about claims and evidence, takes time and practice on the part of the teacher, but the results are clearly worth it!

Initially, students will need practice, too. Students are used to teachers asking factual, knowledge-based questions. These types of questions are the norm in most classrooms today. Students may even feel frustrated when teachers ask questions such as "How do you know?" and "Why do you think that?" because they have not had to answer these questions often, and they will want you as the teacher to provide them with the answers. However, once students get used to this type of questioning, they will rise to the occasion. We have even heard students say, "OK, I know, you're not going to tell me the answer right away, so I need to think again and look for additional information." This is truly a great moment when students recognize that we are pushing them forward and they are willing to work to negotiate their own understanding!

Where Do We Get Questions to Investigate?

After the teacher has identified the core concepts to be addressed—for example, the big idea—it's time to get started. One of the most important things to do before asking students to generate questions about a topic is to activate their prior knowledge about the topic. Activating prior knowledge is critical for a number of reasons. First, it allows you as the teacher to develop an understanding of the conceptions students have about the topic. In addition, activating prior knowledge gives students a chance to conduct a "memory search" about the topic and helps to stimulate questions.

We know that students are in charge of their learning, so we have to determine what they already know before we can begin to create an environment in which we can provide support for their current knowledge and move them to develop new understandings. The most important thing here is to use the information gained from the results of activating prior knowledge to plan instruction. This means that we might have to change the unit to allow for more study or negotiation of meaning in specific areas as determined by the students.

Conducting a read-aloud of a quality fiction or nonfiction book or article is one way to activate students' prior knowledge.

Other ways to activate prior knowledge include:

- ❖ Using a graphic organizer such as KWL (know, want, learn)
- ❖ Using a picture poster to stimulate dialogue and discussion (such as PWIM)
- ❖ Watching a video clip
- ❖ Reading a poem
- ❖ Reading from a newspaper article
- ❖ Watching a videotaped segment of the news or of a program

When activating prior knowledge, our goal is to create a sense of wonderment for the students in our classroom. This sense of wonderment "stirs up" curiosity for students and curiosity invariably leads to questions.

After activating prior knowledge, the next step is to have students develop a concept map to show their understanding of the topic being studied.

Teacher's Voice

Teacher 1: When making a concept map with my kindergarten students, I used color to help organize our map. With our big idea in the middle, I used a second color for each of the main ideas coming off of the big idea. Then I used separate colors for the smaller details to help the kids understand the map better.

Teacher 2: We begin with the topic and from there I ask students what they know. They do an individual map. (In the beginning students didn't have connecting words, but now they do.) The best way for us has been to make a list of words related to that topic and go from there. After they have written all they know, they turn to a partner and share. Then, the two pairs combine with another pair to create a group of four. We then share out as a group of four. One person

Books and Tools

In Figure 5.1, the act of reading aloud to activate prior knowledge can involve text as short as a paragraph or as long as an entire story, depending on the purpose of the teacher, the age of the students, and the content of the material from which the teacher is reading.

Figure 5.1 *An example of reading aloud to activate prior knowledge*

Date: 6-09-05   **District/School:** Any School AEA 13

Name, Grade Level, or Role: Lynn Hockenberry, AEA 13 Rdg. Consultant, Elementary

Title of Book Used: Owl Moon

Pages: All   **Author(s):** Jane Yolen

Concepts addressed from science: "The search for food and the interactions involved in *feeding* are critical if animals and plants are to acquire the nutrition needed for growth and development."

Language arts concepts and processes represented in the text selection: Activating Prior Knowledge

Introduction to the Read Aloud: We have been studying plants and animals and talking about the ways they get the food they need to grow and develop. Today we are going to begin our study of owls. I'm going to read the book *Owl Moon* by Jane Yolen. As I read, I want you to listen for clues to think about the way owls behave or act and where they live—their habitat. I also want you to look carefully at the pictures to see if you notice anything about the owl's body that might help it get the food it needs to grow and develop. I will stop reading from time to time to allow you to write down some notes or draw a picture to help you remember the story and think more about owls.

Read the book, **Owl Moon** *by Yolen.*

Stop at pages marked in book to allow students to take notes or draw pictures about the owls' behavior and habitat and the ways an owl might use its body to help it get food.

After reading the book say, "Now I want you to take a few minutes and think about the book **Owl Moon.** *Look over your notes and your pictures. If you want to add more to your notes or pictures you may do so now. Be sure to think about the way the owl acted, where it lived, and the ways it might use its body to get food."*

*Form adapted from Every Child Reads Material, Iowa Department of Education, 2005, Emily Calhoun, The Phoenix Alliance.

adds to the class concept map, and we keep adding until all the details have been added—regardless of being right or wrong. No judgments are made at this time. The chart stays up and we may add to it as we learn further (with a different color). The students do another map or add to their own at the end (with a red pen or other color). They may cross out any incorrect information at this time. It is surprising to see how much growth is shown. This is so needed for their self-esteem.

From the Students

How do you use concept maps in your class? I begin a new unit with the class making a group, pair, or individual concept map of their current science concept, for example, plants, soil, and electricity. This map reflects where the class is in their current understanding. I often use sticky notes to brainstorm any words associated with the topic and then put the words into a concept map, joining words and ideas that tie together. After new learning, we revisit the maps and change any misconceptions or add new knowledge. Concept maps are a good place to introduce vocabulary used in the unit and keep key concepts posted and visible throughout the unit.

Figure 5.2 *A fourth-grade classroom's ongoing concept map*

A concept map is a tool to help teachers make instructional decisions. Concept maps help the teacher to decide:

❖ What do the students know?

❖ What core concepts are missing?

❖ What misconceptions can be identified?

❖ What concepts are connected?

❖ What instructional decisions could one make?

Look at the concept map diagnostically, thinking about how to focus instruction on the areas where students have misconceptions or where they are missing key concepts that relate to the big idea of the unit. The ultimate goal is to help students negotiate understanding of the big idea, and the concept map is an ongoing tool to help gather information about students' current and developing understanding.

The concept map leads to questions from the students about the topic. As students begin to ask questions, we record them for students or we ask them to write the questions on sticky notes. In SWH classes, we often hear, "Wow, that's a great question!" "Let's write it down." If you use a KWL (know, wonder, learn) graphic organizer with students, this is a good place to record students' questions.

A question board in the classroom is another great place to record those questions (Pearce 1999). Many SWH classrooms have a question board where students write questions on sticky notes and post them for consideration. A question board can be a bulletin board in your classroom titled, "Questions We Have." If bulletin boards are not available, posting a sign titled "Questions" on a door in your classroom also works. Some teachers simply take a piece of chart paper and post sticky notes or write down students' questions. Primary-grade teachers can record the questions for students. This is a great way to help primary-grade students see the connection between speech and print.

Another strategy teachers have used was adapted from the work of Wohlwend (2004) where we organize our questions around nice to know, need to know, and essential. Teachers have created large charts with these three concentric circles or boxes. Students write their questions about the topic on sticky notes, which are then placed on the chart categorizing them as nice to know, need to know, or essential. The discussions are grand, and we often find the one or two questions that we identify as essential often are or relate directly to our big idea on the topic.

HAVE A GO!

Think about the previous examples of activating prior knowledge, including the use of the concept map. How does activating prior knowledge stimulate curiosity and questioning? What strategies are currently being used to activate prior knowledge in the classroom? How can the information gained from activating prior knowledge assist in determining the instructional needs of the students? See Appendix C to explore these questions.

How Do We Help Students Ask Questions That Are Worth Investigating?

Teaching students about higher-level thinking by using the Bloom's Question Starters as a tool can help students to think about the kinds of questions they are asking. Students can be taught to identify whether the questions require facts or knowledge answers or if they require opinions, evaluations, and further justification.

Questions can be coded as *thick* or *thin* questions (McLaughlin and Allen 2002). *Thick* questions are those that are essential to help negotiate understanding. They relate to the big idea and require time and critical thinking. Thick questions involve "digging in deeper" by investigating, researching, or asking experts to find answers. *Thin* questions, on the other hand, are generally fact-based questions that can be thought of in two ways. *Thin* questions may be fact-based, knowledge-level questions that can be an-

From the Students

In this fourth-grade classroom, the students have created a chart to organize their questions into the categories of nice to know, need to know, and essential. In this example, the students come to the board and present their individual questions and then negotiate with the class about in which category the question should be placed. Other times, students write their questions on sticky notes for easy placement and movement on the chart.

Figure 5.3 *A fourth-grade questioning chart*

swered with a yes or no response or by looking in a book and finding the answer in a single sentence or paragraph. They are really "right there" questions. Another way to think about *thin* questions is to think about those questions that the answers are "nice to know" but may not be necessary to fully understand the big idea. Just as in the quote from the third-grade student at the beginning of this chapter, she explores the meaning of "thick" and "thin" questions and points out to us that students quickly begin to see what makes a question "good"—because it encourages depth to our thinking.

Another way to help students ask good questions is to use *question starters*. As students get ready to pose questions, teachers can suggest, "As you start thinking of questions, here are some phrases that you might want to use to help you." The teacher writes question starters such as these on the board or overhead:

- ❖ I wonder if . . .
- ❖ How can . . . ?
- ❖ I wonder whether . . .
- ❖ What if . . . ?
- ❖ How might . . . ?
- ❖ What affects . . . ?
- ❖ How come . . . ?
- ❖ Does . . . ?

Question starters such as these help students to phrase questions as well as move away from the yes/no questions to those that will require additional thought and investigation.

This is also a good time to talk to students about the mechanics of writing questions. Teachers may say, "As you write your questions, let's remember what we know about questions. How do we begin a question?" (With a capital letter.) "What punctuation mark is at the end of a question?" (A question mark.) These simple reminders can help students see how literacy, in this case, writing, is a part of everything we do.

Teacher's Voice

I have taught hands-on science for several years. Since implementing SWH in my classroom, I have observed that the excitement about science increases when students are allowed to formulate their own questions and design their own experiments. Before SWH, if my students had a question, I would give them the answer or find a source for them. Now I allow my students to find their own answers through experimentation or research. This has made them more responsible for their own learning and has made them better problem solvers. Some things to keep in mind:

- ❖ Know that the kids' questions may be hard to answer. Post them and have students search at home for answers as well. Make it a game.

- ❖ Don't forget to revisit unanswered questions or show them what they thought they knew in the beginning. It is really important to them and sticks with them.

- ❖ Ask questions, don't give answers. Answer a question with a question and point out resources.

What's the Difference Between Researchable and Testable Questions?

After questions have been posted on the question board, the teacher and the class decide together whether the questions are *researchable or testable*. *Researchable* questions are those questions that we cannot test in our classrooms or own environment due to equipment restraints, space restraints, or time restraints. These questions can be very powerful for students. Researchable questions are investigations in and of themselves, which require students to analyze, synthesize, and form opinions. Students have to look to the experts and decide if the experts' opinions are valid and supported by data, or if the experts are simply expressing an opinion.

Often, researchable questions are those questions that lead you to text. This text could be a nonfiction book in your classroom, the textbook, an encyclopedia, or the Internet. Researchable questions sometimes can be found easily in a book or they can be questions that are going to require time to investigate thoroughly. Questions that require research are great opportunities to incorporate literature in science. Students read, investigate, write, think, and ask additional questions as they research. Asking outside experts can also be done through interviews, letter writing, or emailing. All of these tasks are authentic real-world activities that engage students and help them negotiate meaning about the big idea.

Teacher's Voice

Teacher 1: After students shared their questions about the topic, I had the class decide if each question was researchable or testable, and then we put that question under the correct heading on the board next to our concept map. The testable questions were where our investigations began. I dealt with the researchable questions by letting students choose a question to research. They then went to nonfiction books to locate answers to the questions. Students had to find answers from three different sources. This allowed students to see if authors or experts agreed. Some students found authors didn't always agree and, therefore, this led to further discussions. After their research, students shared the answers with the rest of the class.

Teacher 2: I use concept mapping, KWL charts, and a pretest to gather prior knowledge. From these pieces, the students generate questions they have about a concept or idea. The questions can be generated through a group discussion, in small groups, or individually. In my classroom, we share any question and post it around the room on a chart. We then have a discussion as to whether the question is testable or researchable. I have the students star the questions they can test. We try to answer these questions through a lab experience; the researchable questions can either be answered by reading as a class what the experts say or through their own reading of any nonfiction texts. They write the answer on a sticky note, place it by the starred question, and share these findings with the group at a later date. I also have them put the book and the page the information was found on with the note so any other students can look up the information at a later date.

Testable questions are those that will allow students to actively engage in and conduct investigations. We consider testable questions to be those that we can test in our classrooms, given the equipment or materials we have available. These questions relate directly to the big idea and are necessary for negotiating understanding. Testable questions are then written on the student template under "What questions do I have?" In primary classrooms, or in the initial stages of implementing the SWH approach, teachers may elect to "choose" the first question to be tested. Another way to decide what question to begin with is to take a class vote. Teachers can also choose to allow each group or pair of students to test a different question from the question board.

What if none of the questions posted can be tested? This is a valid question. As a teacher, we are also part of the classroom community. We can write questions for the question board at the same time that the children are writing questions. In preparing for the unit and thinking about the big idea, we may have in mind a question that is *testable*. Keep this question in mind, record it on a sticky note, and place it on the question board as the students are writing questions. This question may or may not be the one that the group decides to test, but it provides the opportunity to ensure at least one question on the board can be tested. This may be necessary only in the beginning phases of implementation of the SWH approach with students. As students become better at asking questions, they will write questions that require testing or investigation. Remember, there are many different ways to initiate these activities.

Teacher's Voice

Third Grade Teacher: I ask the kids to generate a list of questions they have about a topic. As a group, we publicly share the questions and record them on an overhead or chart paper. The groups then discuss (negotiate) whether the questions are testable or researchable. We then negotiate the focus of our investigation; we determine which questions would be the "best." We may decide to focus on one question, or as a whole class we may decide how investigate a variety of different questions. The kids write *T* by testable questions and *R* by researchable questions. I have also asked each group to select one testable and one researchable question to teach during an investigation about a specific topic. It is difficult to address all the questions that the kids generate. I'm still struggling with how to manage this. The questions are so intriguing we want to investigate them all.

Fourth Grade Teacher: I have started with a think-pair-share activity about the solar system. This is a great way to get students thinking about the topic. Then, after they all have a chance to share I ask them to write questions on sticky notes and bring them to me. I then read the question to the class, and we discuss what type of question it is: A testable question is one we can do an experiment for, and the other, a researchable question, is one that we have to research to find the answer. It takes modeling at the beginning, because usually there are only one or two testable questions out of the forty a class submits. We discuss how we could change a researchable question to a testable one. Students will become very active in the process of creating those testable questions.

Some students do have a hard time creating testable questions so we use the questions "How can we test this?" or "What would we do here in our classroom to find the answer?" Sometimes it leads to discussions that someone could test elsewhere (such as NASA), but we cannot test it here. Great discussions come out of that, and it really helps students create questions that we can try to find the answers to. Researchable questions are kept on a chart so that when students are "checking the experts" they can explore their initial questions, and hopefully some of them will even fit into the big picture of the big idea.

Key Understandings

Developing good questions takes time and practice. Understanding Bloom's Taxonomy and using tools such as the Bloom's Question Starters can help us develop questions and move students to higher levels of thinking as they negotiate meaning about the big idea. Activating prior knowledge is essential to developing good questions. When students are curious about a concept, questions flow naturally. A good question is one that requires students to think critically and investigate thoroughly, and leads to negotiation of meaning and a deeper understanding of the big idea.

CHAPTER 6

Good Questions Lead to Evidence

I think the SWH is very cool because some people don't think about evidence. With the SWH system it makes people think. And from my experience, I learn faster.
—*A comment from a fifth-grade student*

Turn on the television to any major network on any given night, and you will find a plethora of criminal-investigation shows. It seems we are obsessed as a television-watching nation with shows that deal with crime. The underlying theme to all of these shows is: "What is the evidence?" The actors who play the roles of the criminologists, police detectives, and crime scene investigators are constantly looking for facts and clues—*the evidence*—to help them solve the crime. They ask questions, investigate, make an initial claim about "who did it," ask more questions, ask experts, research, and investigate further until they find the patterns of evidence that lead them to a conclusion and a claim, which of course, solves the crime.

When we are conducting science investigations, the process we want students to engage in to negotiate meaning is very similar to the process that can be seen nightly on television. We want students to question, investigate, make a claim based on their evidence, share their claim and evidence with their peers, listen to the claims and evidence of other peer groups, look for patterns of evidence, find out what other experts say, ask more questions, and reflect upon their ideas.

In this chapter we explore how we take the good questions that we developed in Chapter 5 and use those questions to find evidence to answer those questions. In a step-by-step manner, we examine the following frequently asked questions:

❖ We have our questions, now what?

❖ How do we get our students to write a test to investigate?

❖ How do we get our students to be good observers of their tests?

❖ How do we get students to write what they observe so they can communicate with others?

❖ How do we get students to understand what is evidence and what is opinion?

We Have Our Questions, Now What?

As we discussed in Chapter 5, a good question is one that requires students to think critically and investigate thoroughly, and leads to negotiation of meaning and a deeper understanding of the big idea. In the beginning stages of implementing the SWH in elementary classrooms, it is often helpful to take a class vote about which question will be investigated. This is especially true in the primary grades, where students will need modeling and guided practice to help them to understand the process of questioning, conducting investigations, finding evidence, and making claims. As students become more comfortable with investigating questions, many investigations can occur at the same time in the classroom.

Once a decision has been made about which question to investigate, it is time to begin. We have found it to be important for students to record their initial understandings about the question at this step because it helps them to focus on what they already know and see how their understanding is deepened and perhaps changed by the end of the investigation. The graphic organizer in Figure 6.1 is used by teachers to help students record those initial thoughts. This organizer will be discussed again in Chapter 8 as we continue the process and examine how students negotiate their understanding of the big idea. Primary teachers might wish to make a class-size graphic organizer similar to this one and record students' beginning understandings. As students share their beginning understandings and teachers record their thoughts, it is a good idea for the teacher to write the students' initials or name next to the beginning ideas to help students see how they have negotiated meaning during the process of the investigation.

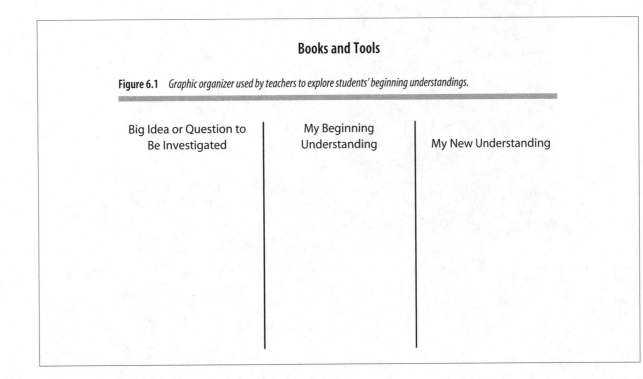

Books and Tools

Figure 6.1 *Graphic organizer used by teachers to explore students' beginning understandings.*

Big Idea or Question to Be Investigated	My Beginning Understanding	My New Understanding

From the Students

In this fifth-grade classroom, the students are studying "preferred environments" as part of a unit on biomes. During this beginning-of-the-year investigation, in an attempt to help the students understand the SWH process, the teacher had the students negotiate the first question to investigate together, which is, "What conditions do darkwing beetles/isopods need to survive?" With this big question in mind, the students think through ways to design an experiment to test this question. The students then work in groups of three to test different variables. As this unit grows, the students then begin to study the preferred environments of different biomes. In Figure 6.2, one student shares her learning about the biome by creating a travel brochure to inform the reader of all the "preferred characteristics" of her biomes.

Figure 6.2 *Fifth-grade student's biome travel brochure*

The Fascinating Tropical Rainforest

136022

Climate

The yearly amount of rain that the tropical rainforest gets is 200 to 1,000 cm. The average temperature is 20° to 35°C. The rainforest doesn't have seasons. It has wet and dry days, it rains most of the time.

Resources

One resource is the wood that comes from the trees. It can be used to make furniture, school supplies, buildings and much, much, more.

Figure 6.2 *(Continued)*

Grab your camera and pack your bags and on down to the Tropical Rainforest. Forget bringing a coat because the temperature can get up to 94°F. You'll want to bring bug spray and an umbrella, because it is at the time of year when it is going to rain. Stay at our Toucan Motel with an indoor and outdoor pool with a hottub included. If your feeling like you just need a break from all of the excitment, you can get a massage for only $90.00. We have many fun activities and long and short hiking trails. The Toucan Motel has computer access and cable color T.V. with air conditionin too. We also have mai restaurants with all different kinds of food. So come on down to the tropical rainfores and it only costs $400.00 for a week.

continues on next page

Figure 6.2 *(Continued)*

Many teachers record questions and beginning understandings on the SWH template (see Figure 6.3). The SWH template is a tool to help students negotiate meaning. One example of a template that can be modified for use in either primary or intermediate classrooms follows. The template can be expanded so that each section of the template is on a separate page; that way, students have large spaces in which to write and/or draw pictures of their work. (Full-size reproducible is provided on pp. 172–73.)

Primary teachers can initially do all the writing for students and use a class template on an overhead. Regardless of what template the teacher uses, teacher modeling of the use of the template is essential to its success as a tool for recording information and helping students to negotiate meaning.

Using the template as a tool to negotiate meaning is another opportunity for students to engage in writing. Teachers can easily incorporate the mechanics of writing while working on the SWH template, as well as provide opportunities for students to write to learn. In one SWH classroom, a fifth-grade teacher said, "When we are writing in our template, what are some things we need to remember?"

The students responded, with the following comments:

- ❖ "Use capital letters."

- ❖ "Put a question mark at the end of your question."

From the Students

Figure 6.3 *The SWH Template Tool*

My name is ________________

My beginning understanding is:

My question is:

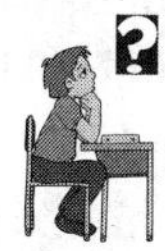

This is the test(s) I did to answer my question:

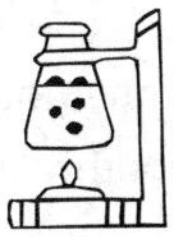

This is what I found when I tested:

My claim is:

My evidence is:

Other people say:

Internal Sources

External Sources

Reflections:

My ideas have changed because:

My ideas haven't changed because:

- ❖ "Write neatly so you can communicate your ideas to others."
- ❖ "Put bullets or numbers before your test steps."
- ❖ "Use a period."

HAVE A GO!

What are the advantages for students and teachers in using the student template as a tool for negotiating understanding? How will you adapt the template to make this tool work in your classroom? Take some time to investigate the use of the template in the classroom. Ideas are shared in Appendix F.

As we continue to work through the process of questions to evidence, we highlight many opportunities to address writing mechanics and grammar as well as the writing to learn that students engage in to negotiate meaning.

Keep in mind that the template is a "tool" to be adapted and used to meet the learning needs of the students and is flexible to also meet the developing concepts of any unit. The parts of the template will never flow smoothly in a perfect linear fashion—sometimes we begin with a claim that leads to an investigation that fuels a question. At other times, we begin with reading, and through reading what others say, we then can develop our own question about the topic.

Teacher's Voice

To make the process clearer for first graders we cut the template apart, place it in their science journal, and introduce it one step at a time. For example, the students are given only the label "claim," and they are responsible for only that one step. After the teacher models how to write a claim the students record their claim. Students then share their claim with a neighbor. We then move to "evidence" and repeat the process. Eventually, the students are able to write claims and evidence independently.

How Do We Get Our Students to Write a Test to Investigate?

Once the question has been written, students need an opportunity to gather the materials they need for the investigation. Teachers usually have a table or counterspace in the classroom where they place many different materials that students might need to conduct their investigation. In the gathering of these materials by students, teachers often discuss with students:

- ❖ Safety issues such as "Do not place any items in your mouth."
- ❖ Management issues to determine which table group or partner group will get materials first. Some teachers use a system in which one person from each group is assigned to be the "Material Gatherer" or the "Go" person to gather the materials needed.

Once the materials have been gathered it is important to give students the opportunity to explore them for a few minutes and think about ways in which they could develop a test related to the beginning question and the big idea. Teachers need to be *very purposeful in relating everything to the big idea* and the beginning question to help students negotiate meaning.

In the beginning stages of SWH implementation, teachers can develop a test procedure as a class. We like to begin this process by talking to students about "Writing a Recipe." Here is what that sounds like:

> Boys and girls, we are going to develop a test to help us answer our beginning question. When we are developing a test it's important to write down the steps of that test carefully so that anyone who reads the test could understand what we do. It's like following a recipe. My grandma makes great chocolate chip cookies. She has a recipe that she follows. The recipe tells her exactly how much of each ingredient she needs to put in to the cookie dough to make the cookies taste great. One day, I asked her for the recipe. She asked me to write down the recipe, but I made a mistake when I copied it down and wrote three cups of flour instead of two cups of flour. Guess what? My cookies didn't taste like my grandma's. Instead they were really dry and broke apart. When I called her to tell her that my cookies didn't taste right, she asked me to read to her what I had written down. That's when I realized my mistake—I had written down the wrong amount of flour! So, if we want other people to be able to do our test just like we did it, to make sure we all get the same results, we have to make sure we write a recipe—our test—very carefully, and write it in order so that others can follow our test. Scientists often ask other scientists to repeat their tests to see if they get the same results.

This analogy has been helpful for students to think about the importance of writing the test carefully so that others can follow it easily.

Writing the test is another place to integrate writing instruction for students. As the teacher and the students write the test together it becomes a shared writing experience. Using an overhead transparency, the teacher and the class develop the test. Reminding students that the test should help answer the beginning question, the teacher often begins by writing *Step 1.* and asking students "What will we do first?" Great discussions follow these questions as students talk about what they think the first steps of the investigation should be. Teachers often ask students to talk to their partner or their table group before asking them to share what the first step should be. After one group shares their idea for the first step, the teacher might ask other groups if they agree with this step by having them give a "thumbs up" or a "thumbs down" to indicate agreement or disagreement. The teacher continues with this process until a logical test procedure has been established.

As teachers engage in this shared-writing opportunity, it is very natural to discuss capitalization, punctuation, penmanship, spelling, sequence words, and so forth. Writing becomes an authentic and purposeful task for students. When the test is written, teachers might ask students to copy the test on their template. Variations for younger students could include:

❖ Drawing the steps of the test

❖ Providing a typed copy of the test steps

❖ Leaving the test steps on the overhead and asking students to refer to it as they work

Students of any age who have trouble copying or writing can be given copies of the test, or the teacher or peer might assist with the writing task.

Teachers might wish to do a "think aloud" as they model the writing of a test before engaging students in the previously described activity. If students have never engaged in an investigation before, they might be unsure of where to begin. Modeling and guided practice for students can help to make their initial attempts with the investigation successful.

After reading the earlier description, one must wonder, "*This is a time-consuming process. Will we ever get to the actual investigation?*" The answer is a resounding "Yes." Yes, it does take time, especially in the beginning. Anything worth doing well takes time in the beginning. If we value engaging students in authentic literacy tasks and connecting those tasks with science, then it is important that we teach students how to do those tasks. Teaching students how to write in authentic ways, such as the one described earlier, means that we do not have to engage students in worksheets about capitalization and punctuation. Engaging students in authentic tasks in science provides more time for students to negotiate meaning about curricular concepts and big ideas.

Yes, we will get to the investigation. Students need to develop an understanding of the importance of written communication in science. Scientists record tests so that they can be replicated. If we are acting as scientists in our room, we must spend time to carefully record our test procedures.

How Do We Get Students to Be Good Observers of Their Tests?

This is when the fun begins! The test is recorded and students are ready to start following their test "recipe" and begin their investigation. To the untrained observer, this stage of the investigation might look like "chaos." However, to those who understand how we learn (see Chapter 2), this stage would look like what it is—students engaged in negotiating their own understanding. Students are:

❖ Talking

❖ Moving between groups

❖ Examining and manipulating materials

❖ Conducting tests

❖ Asking questions of each other

❖ Asking questions of the teacher

❖ Sharing their excitement as they negotiate meaning

The teacher is:

❖ Moving between groups observing students

❖ Listening to conversations

❖ Monitoring interactions between students

❖ Asking probing and clarifying questions

❖ Providing support to those students who may require assistance

❖ Focusing on the Big Idea

The best way to describe this setting is to think of an orchestra conductor and the orchestra members during an orchestra practice. Each section (group) of the orchestra is engaged. Each group is practicing their instrument, learning their part, negotiating, if you will, the way they will interpret the music. The conductor listens to each section, providing support as needed, moving from section to section, and all the while keeping in mind the big idea—the theme of the music.

Teacher's Voice

From a fourth-grade classroom:

We kept three cages of crickets in our room during a nutrition unit. The kids decided to feed one cage only candy, the other meat, and the third only their natural diet of green veggies. The necessity for proper "fuel" for living creatures was magnified in the crickets' behavior, or lack of. After many cricket fatalities in the sweets cages and lethargy in the meat one, the kids made a claim saying they, too, should eat foods naturally designed to give their bodies energy. We went on to investigate what exactly those foods were.

How Do We Get Students to Write What They Observe So They Can Communicate with Others?

One of the biggest challenges for teachers during the investigation is finding the right balance of support, questioning, and management techniques to create the learning environment discussed in Chapter 5. Using higher-level questions, as discussed in Chapter 5, supports students as they think about what they are observing. One technique that works well to help keep students focused on the observation and how it relates to the question and the big idea, and engage them in writing to learn is Stop, Think, and Write. Stop, Think, and Write works like this:

❖ Teacher determines from observation that students are not recording information about their investigation.

❖ The teacher says, "Let's stop for a minute and think about what we have been observing from our test."

 ❖ Talk to your group partners about:
   • Are we answering our beginning question?
   • How does our test relate to our big idea(s)?
   • What have you noticed as you are testing?

 ❖ After the discussion in small groups, the teacher says, "Write down two things (or one or three) that you have observed."

❖ Now continue working.

❖ Modification for younger students: Draw what you are observing from your tests.

Stop, Think, and Write can be used periodically during the testing process or it can be used once in the middle of the observation to remind students to record what they have been observing as a part of their test.

Another way to encourage students to write is to have them use charts or graphs to record their work. One teacher we know says, "Be sure to record your observations. Graphs or charts are a bonus to our work today." Before asking students to use graphs or charts, it is critical that teachers model how to use a chart to record data. Using charts or graphs is an authentic math task and provides real-life experiences for students.

All students need ample room for writing and recording what they are observing. For primary students this is especially true. Primary teachers might wish to provide chart paper to students so that they can draw pictures of what they are observing. The small group in which they are working can do these large pictures individually or cooperatively.

HAVE A GO!

Think about your classroom. How do you currently engage students in small-group discussion? How will you blend your current practice with the ideas discussed in this section to help students negotiate understanding of the big ideas through writing and discussion? Explore these questions further in Appendix F.

As students finish their testing, encourage small-group discussions by using Stop, Think, and Write again. Ask students to discuss in small groups: "What did you observe?"

Next, ask students to check their papers to see if they have recorded everything discussed in their small groups. Finally, ask students to pair up and read aloud the observations recorded by their partner. Rereading with a partner provides reading fluency practice, allows for a comprehension check as students read critically to see if they have recorded all their observations, and encourages students to edit and rewrite.

How Do We Get Students to Understand What Is Evidence and What Is Opinion?

As students are observing and recording the results of their testing, opinions about what they think they are seeing will surface. We often talk to students about how scientists observe and look for patterns of evidence to answer their question. We talk to them about taking a "CSI" approach or a "lawyer-like" approach to their observations, asking, "What evidence do you have? What did you observe? Did everyone in your group make those same observations?"

Many teachers have used the story "Mr. Xavier," developed by James Rudd, to help students understand the importance of evidence. (A great way to model fluent reading for students is for the teacher to read this story aloud to hold the attention of and engage *all* students.)

Mr. Xavier

You and your partner are private detectives who have been hired to investigate the death of the wealthy but eccentric Mr. Xavier, a man who was well known for his riches and his reclusive nature. He avoided being around others because he was always filled with anxiety and startled easily. He also suffered from paranoia, and he would fire servants who he had employed for a long time because he feared they were secretly plotting against him. He would also eat the same meal for dinner every night, two steaks cooked rare and two baked potatoes with sour cream.

From the Students

Figure 6.4a and 6.4b *Student use of the template—The first example is from a third-grade student, the second from a fourth-grade student*

Name: _Jeffrey_ Date: _4-19-05_

Beginning Idea...What question(s) do I have?

How do rocks change shape?

| Tests: I tried twisting and smashing it. | Observations: |
| | |

| Claim: My rock changed shape when I twisted it. | Evidence: It broke up in little pices |

How do my ideas compare with others?

they say they twisted it too

How have my ideas changed?

They have because I think watter could change rock

Name: _____ Date: _4-28-05_

Beginning Idea...What question(s) do I have?

What will happen if I put the rock in water?

| Tests: 1. Separate gravel and large peices. 2. Put leftovers in a jar. 3. Add 50 ml water. 4. Stir 10 times. 5. Observe. 6. Let stand over night. 7. Observe. 8. Pour water into flat dish. Observe on Monday | Observations: After stirring   Next day |

| Claim: The big chunks will get wetter and wetter and and break apart | Evidence: before   after |

How do my ideas compare with others?

people can change rocks.

They use machines to do this.

How have my ideas changed?

The rock got soggy so it was soft

Upon arriving at the tragic scene, you are told that Mr. Xavier was found dead in his home early this morning by the servants. The previous evening after the chef had prepared the usual dinner for Mr. Xavier, the servants had been dismissed early in order to avoid returning home during last night's terrible storm. When they returned in the morning, Mr. Xavier's body was found facedown in the dining room.

Looking into the room, you start your investigation. The large window in the dining room has been shattered and appears to have been smashed open from the outside. The body exhibits laceration wounds and lies facedown by the table, and there is a large red stain on the carpet that emanates from under the body. An open bottle of red wine and a partially eaten steak still remain on the table. A chair that has been tipped over is next to the body, and under the table is a knife with blood on it.

After the students have read the story, engage them in the following discussion: *Based on these preliminary observations, please work with your partner to draw initial conclusions about what happened. Please provide as much evidence as you can to support each conclusion you make.*

Primary-grade teachers might wish to provide an alternate form of this story. What is important is that students have the opportunity to think about what is evidence that they can observe and what is opinion. Understanding the difference between fact and opinion is an important skill in reading as well as in science. This is another example of how science and literacy are embedded! Teaching the difference between fact and opinion in the context of science provides an authentic, real-world opportunity for students to practice the reading skill of understanding the difference between fact and opinion.

When students are conducting investigations, teachers need to be purposeful about the types of questions they ask so that the students will think critically about what they are observing. Using questions like these help students to be careful observers of their tests:

❖ What did you observe?

❖ What evidence are you finding?

❖ How do you find this information?

❖ Why did you?

❖ How do your observations relate to the question you started with?

❖ How do your observations relate to the big idea?

Once students finish their initial investigations and record their observations by drawing pictures, labeling pictures, drawing and labeling diagrams, using charts and graphs, or writing in narrative form, they are ready to look at their evidence and begin to make claims. This will be the focus of the next chapter.

Figure 6.5 *An example of a fourth-grade student's use of the SWH template to examine the Mr. Xavier murder mystery*

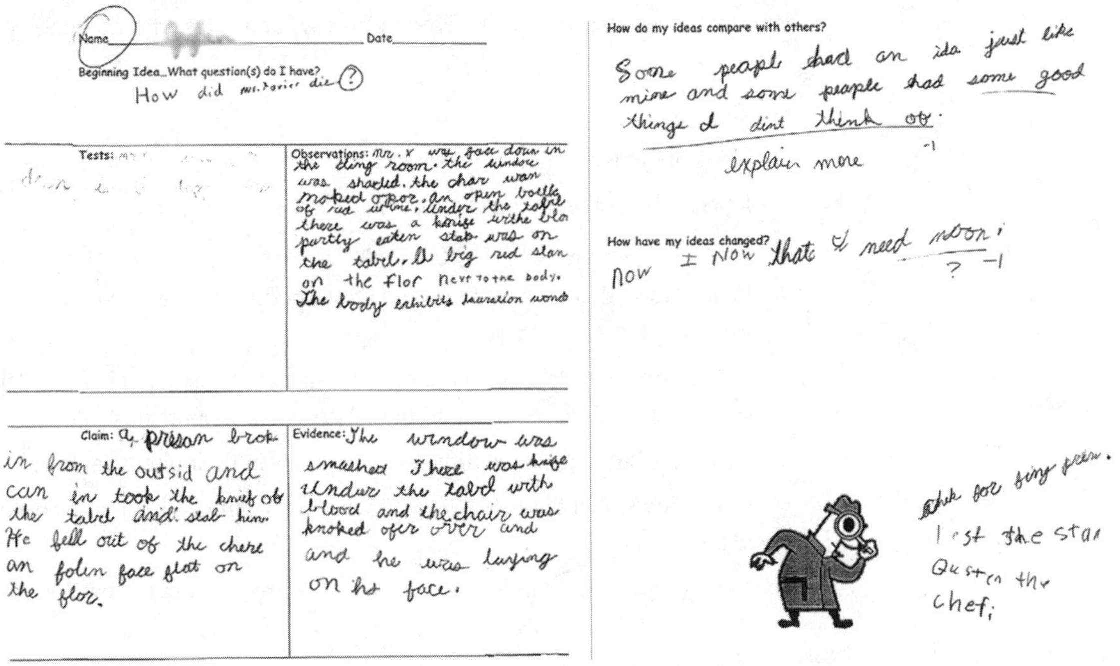

From the Students

Teachers of younger children have often been concerned about using the "Mr. Xavier" murder mystery because of its graphic nature. So, to help them, we enlisted the help of a fifth-grade class to write some "less graphic" versions. One fifth-grade student shares her story:

The Case of the Missing Pencils

Pretend you and your classmates are detectives and you're trying to find two red sparkly pencils. I'll fill you in on some information.

It was a stormy day and the rain was pounding on the ground. The principal said on the speaker that all recesses would be inside (Boo!). So at lunch recess, six-year-old Bri got out four of her red sparkly pencils and one pencil sharpener. She asked the teacher if she could get a drink. The teacher, Mrs. Swan, said, "Sure, but go quickly."

So, Bri left the classroom for about two minutes, and she came back to find two of her red sparkly pencils were gone. Her clues were that there were red pencil shavings on the ground under Jay's desk. Jay had lead smudges on his fingers and red sparkles all over his hands. Now, using the clues, can you make a claim about who took Bri's pencils? What is your evidence?

Key Understandings

Good questions, questions that require higher-level thinking, lead to evidence. The process of students negotiating understanding of the big idea, the process that takes students from questions to evidence, is often "messy" and takes time. Students need to:

- ❖ Investigate
- ❖ Observe
- ❖ Think about what they are observing
- ❖ Discuss their observations with peers
- ❖ Ask questions about what they are seeing
- ❖ Reflect upon their observations and have opportunities to record their observations in a variety of ways

When students are actively engaged in negotiating their understanding through observation and investigation of their question(s), teachers support students by:

- ❖ Observing students to identify misconceptions in their understanding
- ❖ Prompting students to "look again" while providing additional opportunities to investigate
- ❖ Asking additional higher-level questions to help students negotiate understanding of the big idea
- ❖ Providing a safe environment that encourages students to take risks and think critically

Remember: Each of us is different in how we teach, and, thus, how we use the strategies will vary. Keep practicing to build a series of practices that work for you and your students.

CHAPTER 7

What Evidence Leads to Claims?

I like making my own experiments and arguing with other groups about it. I also like making claims and evidence and comparing it to the experts.

—*Comment from a fifth-grade student*

As you read the "Mr. Xavier" in Chapter 6, you might have felt you were quick to form an opinion of what happened to Mr. Xavier. But if you slowed down your thought processes, you would notice that you weighed each piece of evidence. Was it important? How was it related to other pieces of evidence? Your thoughts started organizing the evidence by relationship and logic. Soon, based on the analysis of the evidence, you formed an opinion. Once you were able to articulate the claim, we are certain you felt yourself going back over each piece of evidence wondering if you felt it supported or refuted your opinion. Now, if you were lucky enough to be with a group of people reading "Mr. Xavier," you might have been discussing the evidence presented in the story. As you talked, your opinions might have changed as to the strength of each piece of evidence. You might have even changed your opinion based on the discussions, which would have led you back to the evidence. This entire cycle, which might have taken only moments in your head, consisted of multiple negotiations. Analyzing evidence in order to form a scientifically based opinion, or a claim, is an essential component of the SWH approach.

Teacher's Voice

To begin the year, one second-grade teacher always awakens her students' claims and evidence language by gathering several milkweed pods during the first week of school. She puts one on each student's desk and asks him or her to "wonder" about it. She reads the book *The Wise Woman and Her Secret*, by Eve Merriam, illustrated by Linda Graves (1991), to help them understand the secret of wisdom is, in fact, to be curious. She names what the students are asking about the milkweed pod as questions when Corey announced, "I think it is a SEED!" The teacher pointed out that Corey had just made a claim. But did he have evidence? Discussion was rich as the students tried to decide how they could prove it was a seed. Someone suggested poking it with a toothpick. What happened? A milky substance oozed out of the inside! Was that evidence that it was a seed? Another student suggested cutting it open. Different students decided to cut it in different ways. Jonathan said, "Inside it looks like a bean pod—do you think that is why it is called a milkweed pod?" A new question, a new claim, and new evidence to gather.

How Do We Help Students Analyze Information?

The students have completed their test and collected their data through their observations. Now what? Students need to analyze each piece in order to form a claim. Sometimes as teachers we want to rush through this part—hurry up and decide on the answer. But remember, learning is about negotiation and if we don't let students think about what they've just done, they'll do exactly what they have been told to do—hurry up and find an answer. They might have learned how to complete one more section of the template, but chances are they haven't deepened their understanding of the big idea. So, what's a teacher to do? Slow down!

Think about learning to drive a car. Instruction typically begins with someone providing a step-by-step lesson on how to start the ignition or make a turn. In addition, the instructor talks out loud about the countless decisions being made while driving, "I always watch carefully as I turn this corner because there is a school up the street" or "This light is just turning yellow—I haven't entered the intersection, so I better stop." Driving a car isn't easy. We begin as a passenger and then, under supervision, begin driving. Finally, we become independent drivers, but only after successfully proving to somebody that certain skills were achieved. From there, it takes time as we are constantly refining our skills.

Analyzing evidence to make a claim is a lot like driving. It isn't a skill we can assume students pick up independently. First, it is an invisible process. Analyzing your own thinking as you read "Mr. Xavier" illustrated this point. Teachers can make it visible by talking out loud while they analyze evidence in a whole-group setting. Also, asking students to think out loud while they analyze evidence lets the teacher "see" they are thinking.

As teachers and students think about their evidence they need to consider the following:

- ❖ What question were we trying to answer?
- ❖ What is the big idea our question relates to?
- ❖ What evidence have we collected related to our question and/or the big idea?
- ❖ How is the evidence we have collected related to my question and/or the big idea?
- ❖ Do we see evidence that seems to belong together?
- ❖ How confident are we in relation to our evidence?

If the test was completed as a class, then the analysis of the evidence could be done as a whole group. If the students are pretty new to using this skill, holding the discussion as a class provides the opportunity to model thinking if needed. It also provides an opportunity to encourage students to talk to one another instead of at you, the teacher. The discourse that can happen between students of all ages is a powerful learning tool. Analyzing which pieces of evidence are connected or related can be great conversations between students! The students will become very passionate when trying to defend the strength of their evidence.

Teacher's Voice

A second-grade teacher shares her classroom story of argumentation:

Emma is a good student: bright, kind, and positive. She is polite and pretty quiet. As we discussed our findings after dissecting flowers, the discussion included "nectar." In her sweet, polite voice, Emma told her best friend, Mackenzie, "I disagree with what you said about nectar." She continued on explaining her rationale for disagreeing. Mackenzie listened attentively and then proceeded with her rebuttal. All of this took place with no input from me. This seemed to give license to other students to disagree constructively. It's beginning!

Teachers also have used this opportunity to break into small groups. The test and collection of data may have been as a whole class, so breaking into small groups to analyze data might be a perfect time to give students practice in negotiating with fewer people. They get to participate in the discussion more because there are only four people involved instead of twenty. In addition, they'll have a chance to hear how the other groups analyzed the very same data. This helps to broaden their understanding of how two people can look at the same evidence and come up with two very different claims—as illustrated by "Mr. Xavier."

Another alternative for analyzing the evidence is letting the students work independently. Often teachers will have the students examine their evidence silently first before moving into their small group or beginning a large-group discussion. Students get a chance to organize their thoughts and get ready to share.

The answers to these questions will help to form a claim based on the evidence. Once students do decide on their claim, the evidence needs to be examined once again. Keep in mind, this analysis and claim formation can be done privately, in a small group, as a whole-class discussion, or in some combination of the three. Teachers again need to foster cognitive collaboration—give students time to talk to one another and negotiate their understanding.

What Exactly Is a Claim?

The answers to the research questions will help to form a claim based on the evidence. As stated earlier, a scientifically based opinion, or claim, is an essential component of the SWH process. A student, or a group of students, analyzes her evidence for the purpose of forming a claim. This claim can be written on a template

HAVE A GO!

Take a few moments to examine how you can put claims and evidence to work in your own classroom. Our claim is that by visiting Appendix E, you will find many ways to get started.

From the Students

In Figure 7.1, the students are using their classroom writing strategies to present their learning after an SWH investigation on balance and motion with a shared-writing experience in this second-grade classroom. On the chart tablet, the teacher and students begin with webbing what they know and can include in their writing about balancing. After the students have brainstormed their details, they construct their story paragraph together as a group, and the teacher records it on the chart paper. This story is then typed on a computer and each child is given a copy of the story (as seen in the figure) with a blank sheet of paper to illustrate their understanding by creating a diagram or image from their own investigations. These are then put on display or placed in a class book. Other times, they are sent home immediately so students can share their developing understandings with family members and friends.

Figure 7.1 *Group-writing opportunity with claims and evidence in a second-grade classroom*

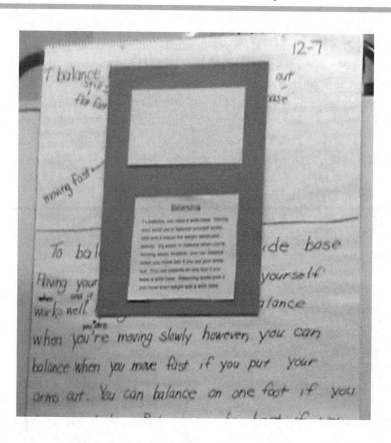

or in a science journal. One alternative is for each group to record their claim and its supporting evidence on a piece of chart paper (see Figure 7.2). This will aid in their sharing of their claim and evidence. Sharing a claim and evidence with other people, or groups of people, is another negotiation opportunity we will discuss soon.

Once students do decide on their claim, the evidence needs examining once again. Teachers need to foster cognitive collaboration—give students time to talk to one another and negotiate their understanding. The role of the teacher during the formation of the claim is often one of a negotiator. A negotiator helps move the process of consensus

From the Students

In one classroom, the students were engaged in a study of matter. One day the class was working collaboratively to examine the characteristics of matter. Each student had made a clay sculpture, and they had gathered together at one desk to begin to describe the characteristics of a solid. Morgan exclaimed, "Look at all this STUFF on my desk."

Her teacher happened to overhear her and asked, "So, then, Morgan, what can you claim about matter?"

"I guess I would say that matter takes up space." The group agreed, wrote down their claim and evidence on large chart paper, and before lunch shared their claim with the rest of the class, who agreed that they also had evidence to support that claim.

Figure 7.2 *Students work collaboratively on a group claim*

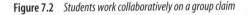

along but doesn't provide the direction it should go. Teachers can ask critical-thinking questions to the student or group to help them make connections but should be careful not to *give* students the answer.

This can be difficult. Because we are adults and have content knowledge, we can see the connections and understandings we want our students to have. It saves so much time and energy if the students can just decide on the "right" answer and reasons for their answer. This is the traditional way teachers like students to pretend to learn. It might be easy, but if you are still reading this book, you know it isn't the best way for children to *really* learn. Students need the chance to analyze their evidence, discuss a initial claim, analyze the evidence again, talk, revise their claim, talk, revise their evidence, talk, write it all down, analyze it all again, erase, talk, write, talk, and the process continues. It isn't easy. It isn't fast. But it is exciting. It is fun. It is *very* engaging. And it *is* the way children learn.

Teacher's Voice

In a kindergarten classroom, the teacher designed an activity to help her young students understand what it means to make a claim and support it with evidence. She began by giving each child a "secret" item hidden in a brown paper bag. To begin, the children brainstormed as a group what could be in the bag. The teacher recorded these "claims" on a chart paper for all to see. The teacher used the term *claim* repeatedly so the children could become familiar with the word. Next, the children were allowed to pick up the bag and set it down. With that bit of evidence, they went back to their chart and crossed off any claims that no longer would apply given the evidence they just gathered. The investigation continued— the children shook the bag, felt the object through the bag, and stuck their hand in the bag without looking. After each test, they were able to revise their claim list. This was a key experience in helping this kindergarten class begin to use the terms *claim* and *evidence*.

How Do Students Share Their Claim and Evidence?

Going "public" can be a scary thing for older students. Younger children are often naturals at sharing their thinking. The sharing of claims and evidence is very *much* like the classic show-and-tell session. Everyone can remember bringing a prized possession to school and sitting or standing in front of all the students in the class. Their little eyes would be glued on you as you told what is that you brought to school and the story behind it. Every time you finished, hands would shoot in the air. Part of the fun was asking the questions; the other part was answering the questions. Many times the teacher would have to call "time" because your class couldn't stop asking and answering questions!

This same excitement can and does happen in SWH classrooms. Taking older elementary students back to the time of show-and-tell will take some purposeful planning on the part of the teacher, but it can happen. A climate of trust has to be created. All ideas have to be honored and respected. Students have to be made aware that one of the jobs of scientists is to put something "out there" for other scientists to question. It is an authentic and powerful process.

So now that the students have a claim and evidence, they are ready to go public. Younger students usually gather together on the floor while older students stay in their desks or at their tables. One student or group at a time shares their claim and evidence, often using a poster as a visual aid. Teachers often ask the non-presenters to:

- ❖ Listen politely
- ❖ Question critically
- ❖ Offer suggestions

From the Students

The first-grade students in this classroom are investigating different properties related to matter. In this writing sample, this student writes in his notebook some of his initial claims about solids and how they compare to liquids and gases. The writing says: Solids keep their shape. Solids are hard to break. Liquids do not have shape. Liquids move a lot. You cannot see gas. Gases are all around you.

Figure 7.3 *First-grade student explores developing understanding about solids, liquids, and gases*

They should be listening for:

- ❖ How the evidence is related to the claim
- ❖ How the claim and evidence are related to the big idea or question
- ❖ How strongly the evidence supports the claim
- ❖ How the claim and evidence are related to their own claim and evidence—the presenters can serve as "internal experts" (more information about this will be shared in Chapter 8)

Teachers often ask older students to write one suggestion or question on a note card for the presenting group to consider. Teachers can ask students to do this individually or as a small group. The teacher collects them. When all the groups have presented, they are handed their feedback note cards. Groups are asked to consider the questions and comments they were given verbally during the presentation, as well as those written on the note cards. Following the consideration, or negotiation, revisions can be recorded on the template or individual science journals. A variation can be to have the group of students write one or more of the suggestions or comments including an explanation of why they did or did not use that comment to revise their claim and evidence.

Recently during an observation in an elementary science classroom, a small group of students sat reading the small pieces of paper that contained the feedback from the other groups that had heard their presentation. Their claim and evidence related to the way birds' beaks are adapted to the food found in the environment. The leader of the group would read each scrap, and we could almost hear the grunts of dissatisfaction from across the room—nobody likes to have their ideas challenged. When listening closer, their comments became clearer. They were adamant that they *had* considered the strength of each piece of evidence and this feedback was useless. Then, almost hesitantly, a student suggested the feedback might have a point. They had not used a set amount of time in their test and that might change their results and, therefore, their claim. The students debated this point for a good five minutes before raising their hands. They wanted permission to revise their testing procedure to include a set amount of time. After some clarifying questions, they began hurriedly to redesign their test. This would have *never* happened if this teacher had not purposely planned an opportunity for the group to reconsider and re-negotiate their understanding.

CHECK THE EXPERTS

Argumentation is a key oral language strategy for understanding that is essential to the work of scientists. We have also found the act of argumentation to be an important component to the work of elementary students in the SWH classroom. Students regularly "go public" with their thinking by presenting their question, research design, claims, and evidence. We have found the work of Jonathan Osbourne, Shirley Simon, and Sibel Erduran (2003) to be very helpful as we examine the ways we help teachers and students to discuss and analyze scientific argumentation.

This preschool student shares her developing understanding on paper during an animal unit. Her claim? The duck is swimming. In her representation here, we see that she is using visual representations in the form of illustrations, and she is beginning to use orthographic representations that look like many of the appropriate letter shapes for what she is attempting to communicate. She can then use this to present her learning to others—her teacher, friends, and family.

Figure 7.4 *A preschool student shares her developing understanding of animals basic needs (Writing says: Duck swimming)*

How Do We Support Students in Talking to One Another?

Making time for students to talk to each other is an essential component of the SWH approach. For a more traditional teacher who prefers to put desks in rows and spend the school day talking at students, it might be a bit uncomfortable to consider letting them do more of the talking. Even more, they need to do more of that talking to each other instead of the teacher. Of course, this doesn't mean that the teacher does not play a role in their talk as well as the learning. Quite the contrary, providing instruction using the SWH approach requires even more teacher involvement. The difference is that the students are doing the thinking, questioning, listening, working, creating, and, yes, learning.

First, consider setting up your classroom so the students are physically in small groups. If the classroom does not have tables, consider moving their desks and chairs into groups of three or four. If this is uncomfortable for your entire instructional day, consider developing a procedure for the students to move the desks at the beginning of their science/literacy block. Think about trying to have a conversation on a plane when the person you want to talk to is two rows ahead of you—it is virtually impossible. Students have to be able to face one another comfortably and have a workspace and common materials.

Second, think about revising the "you may only talk when your hand is up and the teacher has called on you" rule. Of course, we need to instruct and model the skills of polite conversation—giving everyone a chance to speak, not interrupting, and looking people in the eye when you are speaking to them. These skills will be new to many students and they'll have to practice. Provide time to talk about what body language and verbal cues help us have polite conversations.

There will be many times when students must wait to answer after being asked a question. An early elementary teacher uses red, green, and yellow cards to communicate when students should wait to be called on, discuss freely using manners, or think and be ready to discuss. Children learn these cues very quickly. An older elementary teacher uses hand gestures and verbal cues. She tells the students whether she will be calling on them during the discussion. If not, and students still need some facilitation, she'll use her hand to indicate stop to a student trying to interrupt or make a "join in" gesture to someone who hasn't spoken. It has proved very effective in her classroom.

Students might need explicit instruction on how to manage small-group discussions. One way teachers have found to do this is to have students role-play different situations. A teacher can call a group to the front to be the "actors." Their task will be to pretend they are designing a new board game. Two of the "actors" are to agree with one another on the title and one "actor" is to disagree. The actors are to role-play the disagreement. The teacher stops the group and asks the viewers to offer suggestions on possible endings to the role-play situation. The teacher can do this same role-play activity with various scenarios involving as many students as possible. This is really fun for students and they internalize the decision-making process. As real situations or disagreements come up in small-group discussions, teachers can refer to this common experience to brainstorm solutions for the group.

Another strategy for small-group discussion is to alternate facilitators. Many students are natural leaders. The students for which leadership is not a strength can build those skills through this small-group work. We as teachers tend to know our students and which will need more support when it is their turn to "lead" the discussion. One easy way for them to begin feeling comfortable in this role is to simply keep track of who talks. The student can write everyone's names on a sheet of paper that is visible to the group. Every time a student talks, the leader makes a hash mark next to their name. It will become obvious quickly who might be dominating the conversation or who might not be sharing. This is not a judgment. It is data that can help the group make decisions. Is there someone in the group who has expertise in this area? Then he

Students in this third-grade class engage in a cooperative writing experience, which leads to a great deal of argumentation and negotiation as the three female students decide how best to represent their learning during a matter unit in the form of a play. The students were presented with this challenge for their summary-writing experience at the conclusion of their SWH unit—write a play, song, or story to present their learning to others in the class. This was an important act of negotiation and using each other as experts to explore observations, understandings, claims, and evidence.

Figure 7.5 *A play about matter written by a group of third-grade students*

The Girls Club
11-19-04

Scene: The girls met at their clubhouse.

Erica: Since we are studying matter maybe we should take a trip to the rain forest.

Josie: Sound cool!

Lizzie: Awesome!

Erica: Come on then, let's go.

Scene: They started packing.

Lizzie: Let's hit the road.

Josie: But first let's discuss what we're going to learn about.

Erica: Let's talk when we get to the rain forest.

Scene: They started walking and reached the edge of the forest.

Josie: It's now or never let's go in.

Lizzie: Okay.

Erica: Come on Lizzie, don't be a scaredy cat.

Lizzie: I am not a scaredy cat, just watch me.

Josie: Break it up girls, break it up. We're here to study matter and matter only.

Scene: They started walking into the forest.

Erica: Come on let's have a review. What are the three states of matter?

Lizzie and Josie: Solids, liquids, and gases.

Erica: What are the two kinds of matter?

Josie: Living and . . .

Lizzie: Nonliving

Erica: Very good.

Scene: They walked but there was something that they just didn't see.

All: Aghh! Help! We're trapped!

Scene: They calmed down.

Josie: That must have been a solid we tripped over.

Lizzie: Yeah

Erica: Hey, let's climb up that vine. It looks like it's a solid and nonliving.

Scene: The vine moved.

Josie: I think that's a living thing.

Lizzie: I think I know that.

Erica: Then let's get climbing!

Scene: The girls escaped.

Josie: I've had enough matter for one day.

Lizzie: Great idea, how about you Erica?

Erica: Totally!

Scene: The girls headed home and lived happily ever after.

The End.

will probably talk more this time. Is a member more comfortable sharing her thoughts through drawings or note taking for the group? Then she might have fewer marks. Is there a member who consistently talks more than everyone else? Then that student might notice and give other students a chance to talk. If not, the teacher might coach him in asking more probing questions to their peers.

The leader can also use the data to draw out students who are just waiting for an invitation to talk. If the leader sees a classmate who hasn't spoken, the leader can ask that person for her viewpoint or opinion. A technique that can be taught to student leaders who are having problems getting everyone to contribute is the Token Trick. The Token Trick requires everyone to put a token, which can be a pencil or any other common object, in the middle of the table. If someone decides to talk he picks up his token. Now he can't talk again until everyone else has picked up their tokens and the leader starts them over.

Students will not need to use these strategies on a daily basis. They will need explicit instruction when they are new at talking without the guidance of the "raise your hand" rule, but they'll catch on fast. Speaking in small groups is a universal skill. We are not only providing an opportunity for students to negotiate their understanding of the big ideas of science but building skills that will help them become successful citizens of tomorrow.

Key Understandings

The writing that the students engage in while learning through the SWH approach is focused on building argument as well as giving each student the opportunity to describe his or her understanding of the big ideas. The students frame a scientific argument through writing by answering the questions on the various sections of questions, procedure, observations, claims, evidence, reading, and reflection. Remember that students need many opportunities to go "public" with their learning so they can continue to negotiate new meanings and question old understandings.

CHAPTER 8

Claims to Reflection and the Summary-Writing Experience

> I like the SWH process because it is like a recipe. It tells you every bit of information you need so you wouldn't miss out on the big ideas that help you in your thinking and processes. . . .
>
> —ANNIE, *grade 5*

A teacher was talking to Ned, a ten year old, about the need to wear a coat to recess. Immediately he was excited. His body language was big and his voice high pitched. We have all had students like this before—they are ready to jump out of their skin with an exaggerated passion. This young man could not wait to tell the teacher his grandpa *always* said everyone in their family was warm-blooded. The teacher smiled, as you are probably, knowing what was going to come next. He didn't need to wear his coat to recess—he was *always* hot. It was obvious Ned didn't have a full understanding of that scientific concept and was very disappointed when he did indeed have to wear a coat to recess.

Grandpas are definitely important people in the lives of many of our students and often serve as natural teachers. It is vital that students have access to sources of information, both inside the classroom and outside the classroom, that can assist in their ability to construct a richer understanding of scientific concepts.

What Do Others Say?

During the SWH process students need an opportunity to compare their current understanding with what others say. This need often follows an experimental investigation, but it can also result from a question posed on a question board, a question asked as part of the concept map process, a question stemming from a testing situation, or even a question from the teacher. Teachers need to provide opportunities for the students to compare their understandings to what others say. These may take the form of individual or group research, but they should always be followed by some type of group discourse.

"Internal" and "external" experts are two sources of information for students. Internal experts refer to source information that can be gathered from the classroom, such as other students or student groups. We think of internal experts as those people within our class who can help us understand something in a deeper way. External experts include any source of information that does not come from a member of our class. External experts could include speakers, Internet resources, trade books, textbooks, videos, newspapers, or magazines. We have separated the two sources of information purposely to signify the importance of learning from one another.

During the SWH process, students are asked to present their claim and evidence publicly. Teachers often structure this presentation as a whole-group discussion where each group takes a turn stating their claim and evidence. Others groups are asked to listen critically, ask questions politely, and offer feedback. Students independently negotiate their understanding as they consider what the other groups are presenting. They also negotiate in their small groups as they are questioned during their own presentation and when they consider the feedback given after their presentation. This process was explained in more detail in Chapter 7.

This sharing of claims and evidence serves as a source of internal experts. Other groups might have performed investigations a little bit differently but were directed at the same big idea. If students are aware of the big idea and their goal of gaining deeper conceptual knowledge around that big idea, they can listen for information that helps them. Teachers often have students record claims as they listen during presentations, either in their science notebooks or on a template such as the one in Figure 8.2.

Recording claims, if age appropriate, not only supports active participation during the process but allows the students to get in small groups to look for themes in those claims. How are they the same? How are they different? What patterns do we see? What information do the claims give us toward understanding the big idea?

Internal experts can also be tapped during teachable moments. For example, a kindergarten teacher was using sponges to help build students' understanding of the properties of matter. She provided opportunities for her students to develop a rich vocabulary of describing words such as *hard, soft, squishy, holey*, and *crusty*. During an SWH activity in which students had performed an investigation looking at other properties of sponges, one young student had an experience to share where she connected the sponges she saw on vacation with the sponge her mom used in the kitchen. The whole class talked about how those sponges might have been the same and different. Faces were lighting up throughout the room as each student's understanding changed a little as he or she made personal connections. This new understanding would never have happened without the teacher purposely giving the students a chance to use their internal expert as a negotiation opportunity.

External experts refer to information available to students through sources other than their classmates. As stated previously, this could include speakers, Internet resources, trade books, textbooks, videos, newspapers, or magazines. The Internet is a rich and endless source of information for critical readers. Unfortunately, the Internet is not always a reality of readily available information for many teachers. Bringing real-life experts to the classroom or communicating with them through email or letters is highly motivating for young learners. This is often an untapped market for teachers. Many people in the community and academic world are just waiting to be asked—educating students

Figure 8.1 *A fourth-grade student consults external experts by consulting the literature available in her class-room library*

Figure 8.2 *Graphic organizer to explore student claims during group presentations*

Group Members	Claim (usually one sentence)	Evidence (bullet what you think is significant)	Questions (what about the strength of their evidence still bothers you?)

about their passion is something many of them would love to do. Finally, if we truly want to align our teaching with how we know students learn, we can't provide the textbook as the only source of knowledge in a classroom. Teachers *must* provide students with access to print.

Access to print for an elementary teacher means that there must be nonfiction trade books available to students *in* the classroom that stay in the classroom. Because our students come from a variety of back-

HAVE A GO!

Understanding the variety of ways to include reading opportunities throughout the SWH experience is essential. In Appendix G, we discuss ways to get this started in your own classroom.

grounds, it is vital that they have a rich print environment at school. Quality nonfiction texts can provide them experiences that they may not get in their everyday life. Books open up the world to students and expand their background knowledge. If the class is studying life cycles of butterflies, the students and teacher need to have books available on the life cycle of butterflies as well as other animals such as frogs, horses, or owls. If I know butterflies are born, grow, and die, then I need to read about other animals that are born, grow, and die. Teachers can support the transfer of the students' new conceptual understanding to other organisms. Because it is unreasonable to believe we can have that many classroom pets in our classroom, nonfiction books provide a way for students to have that experience of the diversity of living things.

CHECK THE EXPERTS

When looking for good-quality literature related to science, we use the Search It Science database created by Wendy Saul and colleagues (available from Heinemann Publishers), which allows a teacher to search using various criteria (age, genre of book, science content area, author, text features, and the like). The website can be found at http://searchit.heinemann.com/.

If a classroom has adequate access to print, the textbook can naturally become an additional resource used in very much the same way as the other nonfiction books. Students, while investigating a relevant question, can use their textbook to help them examine "What do others say?" This creates purpose for their reading and resulting writing. Their natural curiosity to explain the situation increases their comprehension of the material. You'll find students read much more carefully and are able to think critically about the material. The knowledge-level facts, instead of being the end objective, become pieces of evidence students naturally integrate into their conceptual understanding. They pick up the scientific vocabulary because they want to be able to decide if "what others say" is close to what their results were—and the only way to do that is to understand the vocabulary being used.

A *think aloud* is a great way for all learners—especially younger students—to participate in finding out "What do others say?" The teacher finds a passage or a page from the textbook or quality nonfiction trade book that answers or supports the answering of the question. As he reads, the teacher shares his thinking. It makes the invisible process of thinking visible to the students. They can actually hear their teacher thinking! By showing your thinking during a think aloud, students can hear how you found an answer that was text based or how you had to make connections to what you already knew. Figure 8.3 shows how one teacher used a think aloud in her classroom.

Figure 8.3
An example of a think aloud

**Example of a "Think Aloud" Focusing on Questioning
Written by Lynn Hockenberry**

Article Used for Think Aloud: "Was 'Iceman' a Murder Victim?" **Author:** Tim Friend, *USA Today*. Article appeared in the *Des Moines Register* on Tuesday, August 12, 2003.

Introduction:
In the month of October, I often think of spooky stories and mysteries. Mysteries always inspire me to ask questions. I feel like a scientist on the TV show *CSI* when I think of mysteries. They make me *wonder* what will happen next. Today as I read this article from the *Des Moines Register* titled, "Was 'Iceman' a Murder Victim?" I am going to stop periodically and share my questions with you. I'm going to write my questions on the overhead as I'm reading today to help me remember my questions as I share my thinking with you. Good readers, just like good scientists, ask questions when they read, especially when they are reading mysteries.

Read: "The 5,300-year-old 'Iceman' discovered in 1991 in the Italian Alps was killed by one or more assailants in a fight that lasted at least two days, according to evidence obtained by sophisticated DNA testing and old-fashioned detective work" (Friend 2003).

Think aloud: **I'm wondering three things here and I've read only one paragraph.** I wonder how they know the Iceman is 5,300 years old? I didn't know that scientists were able to tell how many years ago someone died. It makes me wonder what shape the body was in when they found it? My background knowledge tells me the body must have been in good shape—maybe from being frozen, but I'm just not sure, so I'll have to keep reading and hope to find more information. The last thing I'm wondering from this first sentence is, why do they think the Iceman was murdered? I'm hoping that since the title is "Was Iceman a murder victim?" that if I keep reading, some of these questions will be answered. (As I am asking the questions, I will record them on the overhead projector.)

Note: This process will continue as I finish reading the text. I will stop periodically to share my questions and record them on the overhead projector. After reading the text, I will ask students to work with partners to generate questions about the text. Questions will be shared with the class for further discussion and possible investigation through research.

During or following the think aloud, the teacher might stop and have the students "Stop and Share." The teacher stops reading and has the students turn to a partner and share something new they heard or a connection they are making with their own lives. This might or might not answer the question being studied, but the students are negotiating their new understanding. By stopping to make those decisions, students have to think about what, if anything, this has to do with the big idea. If it does relate to the idea, they should draw or write the new information. Teachers should also help or require the students to cite the source of information.

Students can collect and summarize external sources of "What do others say?" in many ways. Many teachers already might have a system that students use to "take notes" about what they learn. Many SWH teachers use *science notebooks* to collect notes or pictures of what students learn from internal and/or external sources. They can ask the students to include the question and source of information. This helps students not to plagiarize, because at this point, they *are* recording another's thoughts and ideas. Recording "What do others say?" can be independent work assigned to be done at school or home, small-group work where multiple sources are found, or even whole-group work, with explicit instruction on the skills of note taking. In Figures 8.4a and 8.4b, we have included a few templates teachers have used to help students record information they find.

Books and Tools

Figure 8.4a   *Graphic organizer to use while reading*

Your Name and Topic	Question #1	Question #2	Question #3
Source #1	Answer to Question #1 from Source #1	Answer to Question #2 from Source #1	Answer to Question #3 from Source #1
Source #2	Answer to Question #1 from Source #2	Answer to Question #2 from Source #2	Answer to Question #3 from Source #2
Source #3	Answer to Question #1 from Source #3	Answer to Question #2 from Source #3	Answer to Question #3 from Source #3

continues on next page

Books and Tools

Figure 8.4b

Name: _____

My question: _____

My book's title: _____

My book's author: _____

The year my book was published: _____

The author's answer to my question: _____

_____

_____

_____

Page(s): _____

Name: _____

Book: _____

Answer: _____

_____

_____

_____

_____

_____

Name: _____

What could be an answer to our question?

How Have My Ideas Changed?

As stated earlier, to successfully negotiate meaning requires that the learner construct a richer version of the concept; that is, her conceptual framework is different from when she first started. In order to manage that in a classroom, it is *vital* that students record their initial understanding in some way. This can be done on a small scale, looking at individual SWH activities, or on a large scale, to examine a change in conceptual thinking.

After negotiating a question to be investigated, many teachers ask their students to do a "quick write" in their science journals. Given a few minutes, students are asked to start writing and not stop until the teacher calls time. During that period, students record their thoughts about the question to be investigated. What do they already think they know? What do they think they will find out? How do they think this investigation is related to the big idea? For younger students, teachers can coach students in answering these questions and record their responses on chart paper. After completing the investigation, students can come back to the quick write and think about why the investigation worked, what they would change, how their ideas have changed, and what additional questions they have.

Another well-used tool to look at a change of understanding is a KWL graphic organizer. Students write what they know about the question they are asking as well as additional information they might need. After completing the investigation, they can use what they wrote in the Know and Wonder columns to help articulate what they have learned through their investigation (see Figure 8.7).

Teachers can use many other graphic organizers to help students examine their beginning understanding and how it changes through a series of negotiations. Whichever form the teacher chooses to use for this goal, she needs to remember that students need instruction on how to use the tool itself. As with any new graphic organizer or tool, the teacher must *model* and think aloud on its use to scaffold the student, so that the tool moves from a teacher's instructional strategy to a student's learning strategy.

The most obvious and successful way we've found to look at the big-picture understanding is through the concept map students constructed at the beginning of their SWH sequence. The *concept map* asked students to brainstorm everything they knew, centered around the big idea. They were to write one fact or tidbit onto a sticky note and write their name or initials in the corner. Working in a group, the students looked for ways to group the notes, piling any notes that were the same. After grouping the notes by similarities they were to arrange them around the central big idea using arrows and connecting words. The notes, arrows, and connecting words show the current understanding of the group. The teacher can also look at the initialed notes to gauge each student's personal understanding of the concept. The concept map serves as one piece of evidence for the student to look at to determine how his ideas had changed.

A second big-picture view would be through the use of the *pre- and posttest*. So often, we use assessments to give a grade, but we fail to use them as a teaching tool. If students had the opportunity to analyze their understanding before instruction and compare it to after instruction, while thinking about the similarities and differences, testing could become its own negotiation phase. Students might even be able to independently identify—using teacher feedback—where their understanding was still weak.

In this example, poetry erupted in this fifth-grade classroom. As students began to collect their data about the differences between freshwater and marine water, they decided that this type of structured poem would allow them the opportunity to blend their evidence with their words—making a claim. It is an example of how sometimes the form of the writing draws directly from the learning experience and takes shape right in the moment of the investigation.

Figures 8.5a and 8.5b   *Fifth-grade students negotiate meaning through writing after an investigation*

Fresh Water
slow, pure,
raging, moving, flowing,
plants, life, fish, minerals,
rotating, swirling, roaring,
fast, dangerous,
Marine Water

Freshwater
still, calm
singing, moving, speaking
Minerals, life, oxygen, plants
raging, flowing, roaring
cheerful, noisy,
Marine Water

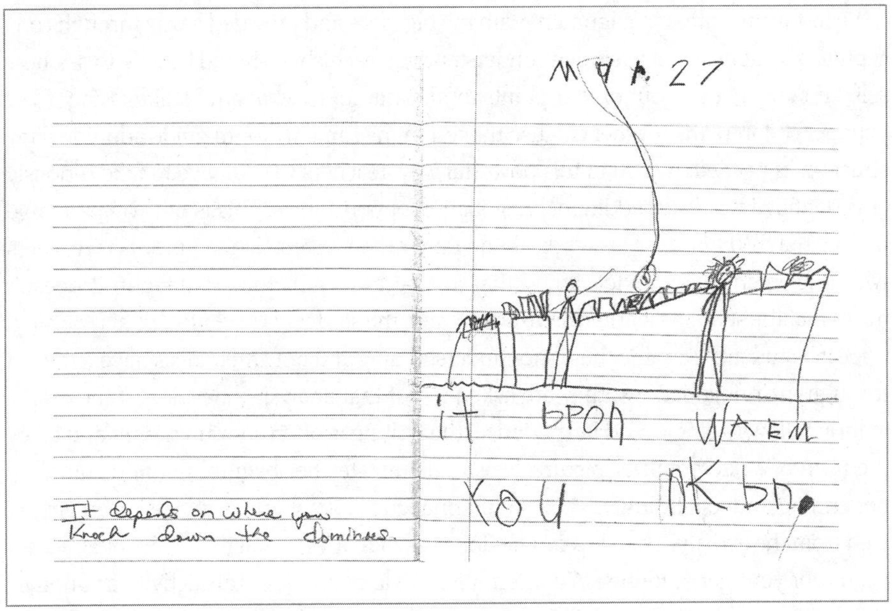

Figure 8.6
A kindergarten student states his new understanding about falling dominoes: "It depends on where you knock down the dominoes."

Books and Tools

Figure 8.7   *Graphic organizer for Know-Wonder-Learn experiences with students*

Question

Know	Wonder	Learn

Another common graphic organizer used by SWH teachers is the following:

Big Idea or Question to Be Investigated	My Beginning Understanding	My New Understanding

If the test were written in alignment with the big ideas and provided a way through conceptual questions to get at student understanding, each child should be able to ask herself, "If I only got two out of four points for this question, what am I still missing?" For younger children, the teacher can use the test in the same way—to guide additional instruction as needed. If used in this powerful way, teachers would have to take seriously any identified needs for additional negotiation opportunities. This is only one example of how the SWH process is a cyclical one rather than a step-by-step process. Teachers who implement this method know that just because something is taught, it doesn't mean that the students learned anything. Again, the student is in control of his learning.

After students examine their prior understanding and how their ideas have changed through their negotiations, they are asked to put that analysis in writing. If the examination follows a single SWH experience, the writing is often short in nature and takes the form of a paragraph or picture. The student states her beginning understanding, her ending understanding, and any additional questions that might have been generated from the activity. This step can be done individually for older students or as a class poster for younger students. We often have students think of this activity as another claims and evidence presentation. What evidence can you cite to support your new understanding?

If the examination follows the completion of unit, students summarize how their ideas have changed toward the big idea through a writing product. The following section details how teachers can support students during this process.

How Do I Summarize What I Know?

As stated in Chapter 2, understanding refers to the ability of the learner to transfer his knowledge to new and different situations. First, he needs to examine what he thought he knew. Strategies to assist students in doing this were discussed in the previous section. Second, the student needs to be able to articulate this understanding to an audience other than their teacher. Having to communicate an understanding to a new audience requires the student to once again negotiate her understanding. The new audience most likely has a different background than the author, so the student must keep that in mind as she creates her writing product. This gives her purpose in her discussions and in her writing.

Teachers can assign an infinite number of products for students to create in order to communicate their understanding. A few are listed in Figure 8.8.

Many teachers use *prompts*, such as the following, to help their students take a specific point of view as they write or create a product:

* ❖ You have been hired by NASA to create a brochure for young people interested in pursuing careers in space exploration. The project manager has asked you to include information on the impact space exploration has on the average American.

* ❖ Your news station has asked you, the chief meteorologist, to prepare a PowerPoint presentation explaining weather patterns. The presentation will be used in a community meeting.

ABC book	Commentary	Graffiti board or electronic bulletin board	Photo essays	Radio program
Advertisement	Diary	Letters—business	Picture book	Scrapbook
Acrostic poems	Dialogues	Letters—persuasive	Plays	Songs—raps
Brochure	Drawings	Letters—friendly	Poems	Speech
Chapter book	Expert interview	Manual	Posters	Travel journal
Comics	Field guide	Newspaper	Multimedia presentations	Speech
Commercial	Flipbook	Online magazine	Question and answer books	Webquest

Figure 8.8
A variety of writing opportunities and genres to try during an SWH unit

❖ Next week is Grandparents' Day at your school. Create a poster illustrating all the ways babies resemble their parents.

❖ Your 4-H club has been asked to do some landscaping around the community fire station. Using what you have learned about plant growth and ecology, write a letter on behalf of your 4-H club to the fire chief detailing your plans for the area.

❖ School will be closing for a month and someone has to take home the class pets! Help your teacher write a manual on how to care for your pets.

The prompt clarifies the audience, purpose, product, and ideas that should be articulated. Also, because of the relevance to the real world and the higher-order thinking skills needed to complete the task, student engagement is increased.

Teacher's Voice

Teachers share stories of how writing increases motivation for students:

Teacher 1: I had a boy in my class who was very rambunctious and was of lower ability than the rest of the students. It was always, "Parker!"—from me, yes, but mostly he annoyed his peers. When we were discussing our class concept map, he had moments of listening to other excellent students mixed with moments of restlessness. But he loved the up-and-around hands-on experiments and was quite vocal about what he tried and what happened. Some of the others were hesitant to act and speak—not Parker. When he wrote in his leaf book, he struggled with sounding out the words he worked to say, but it was all in his picture he drew and took so much time on. This is when he shines. I just hope that his first-grade through senior year teachers give this boy opportunities to shine in science and math, or he will drop out like his two older brothers and end up on the streets.

Teacher 2: In my classroom we do a lot of writing for meaning. Our final writing sample brings everything into view and helps me know what the students have learned. In a unit covering Earth's movements, my students came up with important information that they needed to include and that led them to take more ownership in their writing. In the end we typed up their information on the computer, and it was a great feeling when students were calling me over because they ran out of room. So students learned that they knew a lot more information than they thought—they even had to resize their font to fit it all. In the end a few students had ten-point font and it barely fit!

Teacher 3: To end our forces and motion unit I had students write books. Students were very excited to use the digital cameras. They planned their pictures and text and then took pictures. Pictures were of students throwing footballs, running, pushing someone, tug-of-war, and even the teacher going down the slide. This was a great writing connection to pull their knowledge together. It also incorporated technology! Figure 8.9 is one example from a student's photo book.

Most important, teachers need to remember that this summarization must be process driven. Students need to be provided opportunities to draft, revise, revise, revise, and then finally edit. The revisions need to be focused on ideas, organization, voice, and other characteristics needed for a good piece of writing. Revisions themselves can be negotiations. As students read and reread their product, they'll be wrestling with content and relationships they are trying to express. Editing might happen during the process, but it should also be addressed last to ensure proper spelling, usage, and punctuation.

Figure 8.9
A student's photo essay book on forces

Acceleration is when someone is running then they run faster. Friction is slowing you down when you run.

Feedback is so important! If a teacher has twenty students, then the class has twenty editors to help with the revisions and editing. Students need to be taught the vocabulary to use so the feedback is helpful. "Good!" is not an example of helpful feedback, but it will be the most common if the teacher does not explicitly instruct the class about of the qualities of good writing. Students also need support in developing the questions and comments to prompt the revisions of their peers.

This is an excellent opportunity to mesh writing-to-learn objectives with learning-to-write objectives. You *can* teach students to summarize their new learning while simultaneously teaching them what good writing looks like. Students are motivated to learn how to write because they care about what they are writing.

We cannot stress the importance of teacher modeling enough. If students never see a teacher write and "show" his thinking, some students will never fully understand the level of thinking needed to record their thoughts on paper. Those are the students many teachers claim "can't write." They *can* write; they just need to be shown the thinking that is involved as well as examples of quality writing. When you use a non-fiction book to activate prior knowledge or look up a researchable question, help students notice how the author used her voice to show her enthusiasm or used a specific type of organization so her thoughts were made clear to the reader. Never assume children have a particular skill because it was taught in a previous grade. You know now from reading this book that because something is taught does *not* mean it was learned. Only the student decides what is learned. It is our job as teachers to provide opportunities for students to negotiate their understanding so it finally does reach a level of conceptual understanding. This can happen throughout the entire SWH process, including the summary-writing activity.

How Do I Assess the Summary Writing?

As you start to think about how you will assess your students' writing (or pictures in the case of lower elementary classes), think about your big idea for the unit. Was the information you wanted students to understand fact based? If you focused your instruction on the conceptual understanding of the big idea, it was not. Facts most certainly support the conceptual understanding, but it does not end at that level. A conceptual understanding provides an opportunity for students to show the relationship between facts and the application of those relationships to a new situation.

Teacher's Voice

During a field trip to the university, I gave each of the students a disposable camera. They could take pictures of anything important they wanted to remember about our trip to meet our university penpals, but I also asked them to get at least one picture of a plant that we could use for further investigation when we returned to the classroom. The pictures arrived just as we were well into our plant unit, so it provided another opportunity for the students to pause and express their learning with the written word. One example of a student's writing is shown in Figure 8.12.

The following summary-writing examples are posters from a fifth-grade class that was studying plants. In creating the posters, students had to summarize their findings in a way that grabs the attention of the viewer while providing succinct information. Note the text features used on the posters: bold headings, captions, diagrams, and bulleted text. Integration of technology was used by some students (as seen on the picture on the bottom) while others chose to draw and use their artistic talents (as shown in poster on the top).

Figures 8.10a and 8.10b *Posters about individual student learning in a fifth-grade classroom*

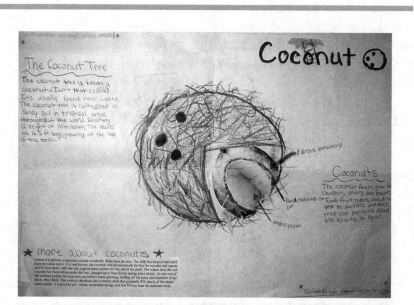

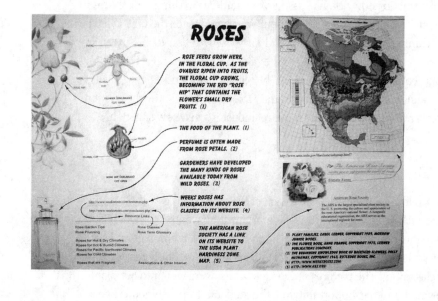

From the Students

In fourth grade while working on our rock unit, students created a flipbook. Each page illustrated and described a type of rock, for example, how the rock formed, where you might find it, what minerals would be in it, and so on. We also had a page dedicated to minerals. This helped the students with writing challenges demonstrate their learning using illustrations and short phrases. I was able to assess their knowledge using this flipbook.

Figure 8.11 *Fourth-grade flipbooks about rock formations*

Many teachers use a rubric to set the target for their students. Lower elementary teachers often use checklists. Many Internet websites provide sample rubrics and checklists. The content of these rubrics or checklists can certainly contain points for participation, collaboration, and presentation, but if your objective was for conceptual understanding, you need to align that instructional focus to your assessment. The evidence for the understanding of the big idea should weigh more heavily than neatness.

Teachers who have been implementing the SWH approach in their classrooms have used various tools to assess the summary-writing experience. In Figure 8.13a, we display one form created by a fifth-grade teacher. She used this form in a variety of ways. Many times, we consider "who" should be doing the assessing. In this case, this was used as a peer assessment so students could respond to each other's "write-up" of the SWH investigation. Other teachers have used this type of form for three types of assessment: self-reflection, peer feedback, and teacher assessment. It is interesting to consider how assessment can come from multiple sources: the student, other classmates, parents, community members, other scientists, and, of course, the teacher. Another assessment tool is shown in Figure 8.13b.

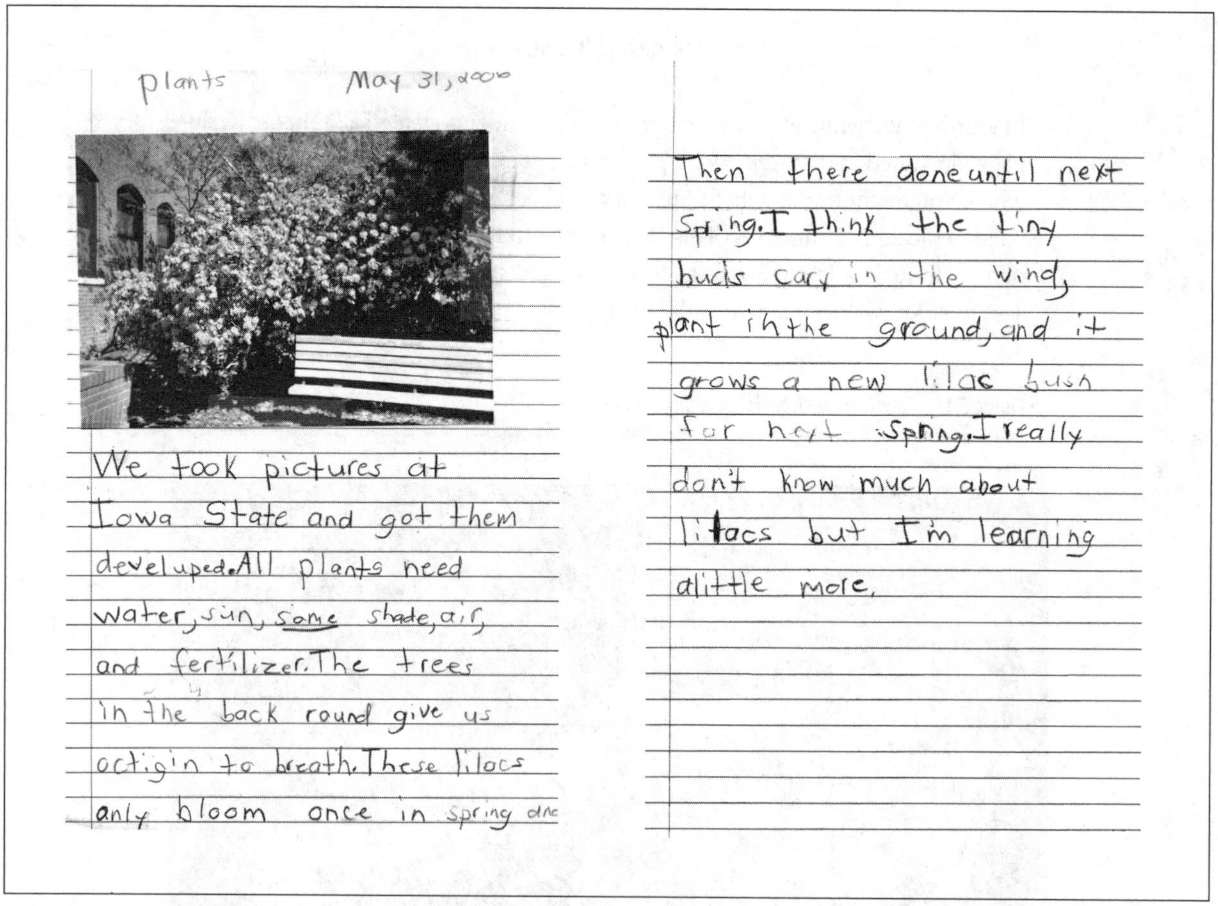

Plants   May 31, 2000

We took pictures at
Iowa State and got them
developed. All plants need
water, sun, some shade, air,
and fertilizer. The trees
in the back round give us
octigin to breath. These lilacs
anly bloom once in spring one

Then there done until next
spring. I think the tiny
buds cary in the wind,
plant in the ground, and it
grows a new lilac bush
for not spring. I really
don't know much about
lilacs but I'm learning
a little more.

Figure 8.12 *A second-grade student's letter about plants at the university*

CHECK THE EXPERTS

Through our work with the SWH and the writing of our students, we have found the work of Vicki Spandel (2004) and the 6+1 Traits of Writing to be a valuable resource. Spandel has created a variety of rubrics that allow teachers and students to look at several aspects of writing and identify each student's strengths and weaknesses. The seven traits include ideas, content, organization, sentence fluency, word choice, voice, conventions, and presentation. Many teachers implementing the SWH approach use these traits to create their own evaluation instruments.

Key Understandings

Students learn by examining what they think, investigating authentic questions, comparing their findings to what others think, and then negotiating their new, deepened understanding. The dialogue and reflection that takes place as a student looks for similarities and differences with her peers as well as credible scientific sources can be powerful. This chapter spoke of the importance of providing students with opportunities to wrestle with their own evidence-based claims, those of their peers, and those of the scientific world. They then used their deepened understanding of the big idea of science to apply it to a new writing situation. The writing products they produce can be a window into their minds. How exciting for the teacher and student! Be purposeful in the time you set aside for students to negotiate their understanding through this process—it will be time well spent. Remember: Many writing opportunities exist—the line between science and language disappears.

Books and Tools

Figure 8.13a *Student Assessment Tool*

Name of Scientist _____

Checked by _____

Please read the SWH and fill in the rubric below.

Description	5	3	1
Overall Neatness/Effort			
Conventions: Spelling and Punctuation			
Understandable Content (Did you understand what we did?)			
Diagrams—Labels— Were they helpful?			

Comments:

Thank you for your time and effort!

continues on next page

Figure 8.13b *Student Assessment Tool*

Matter Letter
Scoring Guide

Name: _____

Date: _____

Clear Explanation
5   Clearly understood
3   Understood
1   Difficult to understand
0   Not Understood

Science Concepts
5   Nearly all science concepts included
3   Some science concepts included
1   One science concept included
0   Science concepts not included

Letter Format
5   Contains all parts of a friendly letter
3   Few mistakes in letter format
1   Multiple mistakes in letter format

Sentence Structure
3   No mistakes
2   Few mistakes
1   Many mistakes

Spelling/Punctuation
3   No mistakes
2   Few mistakes
1   Many mistakes

Signature included
1 point for signing name

Total Score _____/22

Comments:

Figures 8.14a, 8.14b, 8.14c, and 8.14d   *Examples from summary-writing experiences where students used the form of letter writing to express their learning*

Dear, Human,

It's important that you take care of me because you wounden't be very strong. Because I put the right amount of calcium in your bons, and I help your nerve cells.

Your best gland
Parathyroid Glands

Dear Human,

I am the jawbone. I'm writing to tell you that... Well 1, I am healthy, and 2, I wrote to tell you how important I am.

I create the structure of your jaw. Without me, you wouldn't be able to:

- chew your food
  or
- talk to your friends and family

I pretty much support your whole mouth, with the help of surrounding muscles, of course. So, please take care of me by getting lots of calcium.

Your Friend,
(Jaws)
Your Jaw
Bone

5/23/06

Kraft Foods N. America, Inc.
Box SSKATP-8
Rye Brook, NY 10573

Dear Kool-Aid co.:

We are learning about concentration and diluting today. We were making solutions with Kool-Aid. The one that tasted the best was a solution of two scoops of powder and one-thousand ml. of water. Are you going to have any new flavors coming out? Are there any taste-testing groups I could join? Do you make souveneirs? Do you think I could have one? I would like to know about this information so I can be prepared for the new flavor.

2-13-06

Dear third graders,
I learned that friction makes heat energy. Metal is a good conductor. The sun is the biggest producer of heat in the world. Fire is a good form of heat energy, because fire helps us cook hotdogs and smores when you go camping. Heat is good energy.

Getting Started and Examining Our Own Teaching and Learning with Questions, Claims, and Evidence

Figure III.1 *Teachers engaging in dialogue at an SWH summer workshop for teachers*

Whoever teaches learns in the act of teaching, and whoever learns teaches in the act of learning.
—PAULO FREIRE, *1998*

Each summer for the past three years, thirty-two teachers have gathered on a university campus to engage as learners. We have visited the chemistry lab, made rockets, investigated the water quality in a state park, made porridge, and wondered about science, language, teaching, and learning. We have asked questions, made our own claims, argued about evidence, and wrote. Many of the vignettes you have read in this book thus far were jotted on backs of envelopes, torn sheets of notebook paper, sticky notes, and index cards. In fact, in Figure III.1, you see the teachers in action, engaging in an activity called "Chatter Bugs" (Ruggieri 2007). It was the first day of summer workshop and teachers from six school districts had not seen each other since the previous summer, so we began by creating two circles—sitting facing each other. Every three minutes the outside circle would move one chair to the left and the new pair would be given a new challenge: (1) Talk about an aha moment you had this year; (2) Talk about a child who really challenged your thinking; (3) Ask one question that you have about the SWH approach; (4) And so on. We used this dialogue to fuel our planning, investigations, and writing.

This summer we began with a new group of teachers. Some of the veteran SWH teachers joined in on a panel discussion. When asked, "Where do we start with this whole SWH endeavor?" three teachers responded in different ways—their answers intrigued us.

Teacher 1: Ask "why?" It's that simple. You can change your practice today just by going back and adding that one word to your dialogue. So, if I find myself asking a known-answer question, such as what are the parts of the plant, I follow up with a "why do you say that?" Or, I ask, "John, do you agree with what Steffie said?" "Why?" questions are my salvation and helped build my confidence in allowing the kids the power to tell me the "whys" and how things are connected.

Teacher 2: Go back to your classroom and use the concept of "claims and evidence" throughout your curriculum. I started by using it during my read aloud time. "Looking at the cover, can anyone make a claim about this book?" Then, when we finish reading, we check to find the evidence in the book to support our claim. A math story problem is a great question that we can test, make a claim about our answers, and then share our evidence for how we came to that answer. Students soon see that there are multiple ways to provide evidence for any math story problem. I use claim and evidence all through my day—that is how I became comfortable enough to try it in science, where it is natural! And, in the process of my using the terms over and over, the kids picked it up, too!

Teacher 3: My advice? Start with a blank notebook. I mean *blank* and *never* do I, as the teacher, determine what is written in the pages. This was tough because it was a big change for me, but it was one small step that transformed my teaching! Instead of me dictating to them what they should write, every day I make time and ask, "Okay, what do we need to write down today?" Talk about watching negotiation in action! One student will say we need a definition, one will say a list, another wants a chart. Someone will pipe up, "Why can't we just write down what we want to, does it all have to be the same?" Sometimes we will decide "yes" and others "no." But this one small act—giving the power of the pen to the kids—made a huge difference for me when I was just getting started.

With this in mind, the following section is designed to help you create your first SWH unit and to reflect on your own teaching (Chapter 9). Other frequently asked questions answered by teachers in the project can be found in Chapter 10 along with a brief overview about the research that has been conducted on the SWH approach and the impressive impact on student learning. Let's get started.

Implementing Your First Unit and Measuring Your Progress

Teacher's Voice

Before becoming involved with the SWH process, science was never a top priority for me as a third-grade teacher. If we ever had a late start or early out, science was the first subject to go. I think this was because I didn't feel I had much background in science, didn't really understand it well, and didn't feel I could teach it well to the students. Therefore, I was very tied to the book and hoped no one ever asked a question that wasn't in the manual somewhere! When I was approached to be part of this, my first response was, "No—not interested!" When I realized the teachers in the grades before me and after me were doing it, however, I felt that to help with the continuity for the students, it would be in their, and my, best interest to become a part of this "new" way of teaching science. With much apprehension, I agreed to try it.

Since being involved with SWH for several years, I no longer feel science is intimidating. Using this process, where the learning is student-driven, and knowing the students are interested because it is their learning, based on their questions, has made it much easier and more exciting for me, not to mention for the students! If there is something we don't know, we just research it.

I knew I had "made it" as a science teacher when one of the teachers in our school, who is known as the "science person" in the building, walked by my room one day and told me later (to paraphrase), "I saw you having science class today, and the kids seemed to be loving it!" At that point, I knew I had really changed my way of teaching science, thanks to SWH.

Now it is time to have a go with your first SWH unit. When we first began this project with thirty-two elementary teachers, we needed some inspiration. We found it in a children's book called *Ish* by Peter H. Reynolds. In it, a young boy is disgusted by his writings and drawings. None of them look right! He crumples the paper and throws it. However, his little sister grabs it and runs off with it! When he arrives at her room, he realizes the walls are covered with his crumpled drawings that his sister has turned into a crumpled art gallery. A portion of the text follows:

"This is one of my favorites," Marisol said, pointing.
"That was supposed to be a vase of flowers," Ramon said, "but it doesn't look like one."

"Well, it looks vase-ISH!" she exclaimed.

"Vase-ISH?"

Ramon looked closer.

Then he studied all the drawings on Marisol's walls and began to see them in a whole new way.

"They do look . . . ish," he said.

And with that in mind, as teachers, we decided we could try something SWH-ish. "Ish"-ful thinking gave us the freedom to take the risk and try to teach in a way that our students could learn and understand science concepts and also develop language. We now challenge you to do the same.

Putting Together a Unit

The basic outline for a unit follows. This sequence is broad, but it does highlight the essential dimensions of the unit and how we see the flow of the unit going. Figures 9.1 and 9.2 represent two tools we use in planning. The first is a flowchart to use when considering the "flow" of the unit, the second is a chart to consider the language connections that are possible during each step of the SWH process.

Throughout the book, we have asked you to have a "go" with various aspects of the SWH approach. We will reiterate here how to go about getting started on your first SWH unit.

1. Begin by creating your own concept map for the topic.

2. Now consider how you will get the unit started. Remember: The key to beginning a unit is finding out what the students know. Some options for getting this started could be:

    a. An opening activity or centers to help the students explore the topic

    b. Share a variety of books on the topic

    c. KWL charts, PWIM experiences

    d. Debate or discussion based on a key question

3. What investigations and materials do I already have that could support some initial investigations for the students?

4. How can I help students share their learning through claims and evidence?

5. Now consider the language connections throughout the process:

    a. Talking: How will I plan daily for students to negotiate meaning through dialogue and argumentation?

    b. Reading strategies: How will I weave opportunities to read and explore the process of reading throughout the SWH process?

    c. Writing: How will I organize student opportunities for daily "ideating" through writing (consider notebooks and the summary-writing experience)?

6. Assessing learning: How will I know if my students have learned?

Figure 9.1 *Considerations in planning an SWH unit*

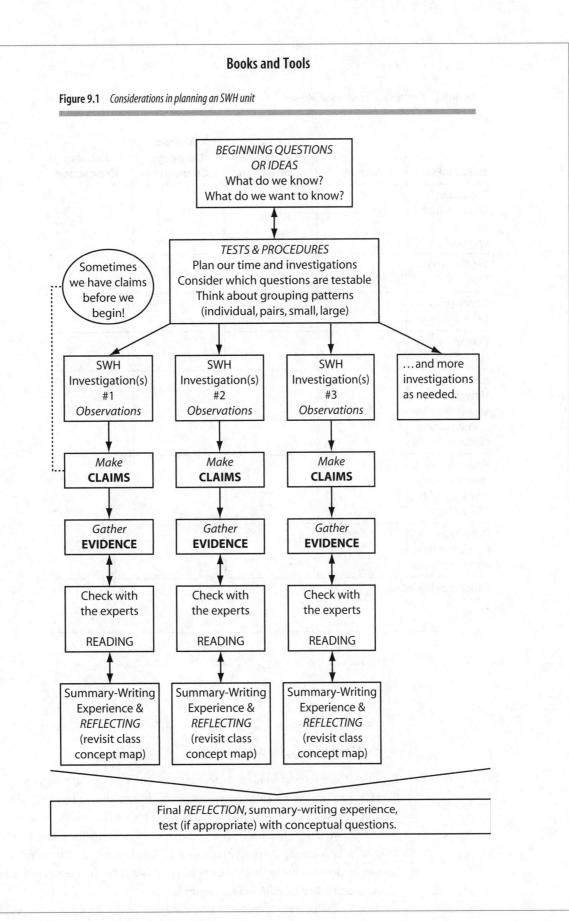

Books and Tools

Figure 9.2 *A tool to assist in planning an SWH unit*

Student Plan	Activity	Oral Language Connection	Written Language Connection	Reading Connection
Beginning ideas—What are my questions?				
Tests—What did I do?				
Observations—What did I see?				
Claims—What can I claim?				
Evidence—How do I know? Why am I making these claims?				
Reading—How do my ideas compare with other ideas?				
Reflection—How have my ideas changed?				

Other considerations:

Teacher's Voice

Teacher thoughts on planning:

Teacher 1: The second-grade teachers plan all our science units together. Since SWH, we are always looking for ways to include literature and writing. We purposefully consider the big ideas and plan questions we can ask the students. Before SWH, we taught from science textbooks and led discussions based on those texts, without planning for student questions. We also now plan more time for our lessons because we know that students will be more active participants in the discussions and activities planned for the units.

Teacher 2: Planning a unit for SWH is different from traditional lesson planning. First I identify the big idea from my district's standards and benchmarks.

Then I make a concept map to reflect my own understanding of the topic. I write a pre- and posttest focusing on conceptual understanding. I collect ideas for activities that could be used in the unit and assemble books and magazine articles relating to the area of study. I think about writing activities that will support the science learning. Once I have started the unit, my planning is done on a day-to-day basis, rather than planning for an entire week or the whole unit at once. This allows me to select activities and plan lessons based on what the students need at the time.

Measuring Your Progress During Implementation of the SWH Approach

After reading the previous chapters and beginning to explore what the SWH approach looks like in the classroom, the question now is, how well are you implementing the suggestions that we have put forward? In this chapter, we will provide a performance matrix that can be used as a tool to examine where you are in the process. This performance matrix is the same one that we use with all of our research into the use of the SWH approach and, thus, represents a large body of work in teacher efforts for using this approach.

The matrix was designed by looking over observations with teachers and attempting to find a way to describe what we were seeing happen in successful classrooms. We began with what we called a "profile of implementation" because our goal was to demonstrate the developmental nature of this learning process—a process that is ongoing and dynamic. We wanted the profiles to reflect this. However, the narrative lists were a bit hard to manage so we consulted the work of Douglas Llewellyn (2001) and appreciated the table format of his rubrics for becoming an inquiry-based teacher. We moved to this table format but chose to specifically focus on four essential traits that we have seen emerge in successful implementation of the SWH approach.

Before we talk about what skills and strategies that we need to concentrate on when implementing the SWH approach, we must talk about the time it takes to engage in this process. With all the teachers who have been a part of previous SWH projects, all have found that change is slow; that is, it is not instantaneous or linear—it takes time to adjust to new strategies. Change is not instant; there is no sudden movement away from one style of teaching to another, and some days just go better than others. The process is truly an example of the two steps forward, one step back cliché. We have to change some of our thinking, change how that thinking transfers into the classroom, and then respond to the changes in the classroom that result. To make matters worse, as you start out with simple changes, the complexity of all the changes meshed together makes you realize the difficulty of the whole process. However, the end results are certainly worthwhile, so fight the urge to say that this process isn't worth all the effort. Despite the difficulties and effort to move to a classroom that is moving toward a "practicing level," it is quite energizing both personally and professionally.

Before moving into the skills and practices involved, we would like to remind everyone that management is a critical component of the SWH—or any inquiry—approach. Although we are promoting student-centered learning strategies, this does not mean that the teacher does not have to deal with management. As discussed previously, we need to manage behavior, materials, and the curriculum. All the skills and practices we talk about in the following paragraphs require good management strategies. Remember: Setting up a nonthreatening learning environment where all students are able to participate requires that good and meaningful management strategies are in place. Student-centered does not mean a lack of effort on our part as teachers; rather, it will take more effort on our part. But the rewards are worth it.

In trying to determine how we can best help teachers improve their practices, we have developed a matrix with four major skill areas that we use for classroom observations and four categories of success. These categories are:

❖ Beginning: This level is where the teacher is beginning to investigate the strategies. While they are Beginning, they tend to keep the major focus on themselves as teachers rather than on the students.

❖ Approaching: This level is where the teacher is beginning to build the skills and is attempting to use them on a more consistent basis. The major focus is occasionally the student.

❖ Understanding: This level is where the teacher is beginning to move away from teacher-centered practices, being more consistent in implementing the required skills, and shifting the focus to the student more often than to the teacher.

❖ Practicing: This level is where the teacher is consistently using student-centered practices and the focus is primarily on the student.

As we outline the following matrix, remember that as teachers we are constantly moving between these categories. We constantly adapt and change actions as the lesson unfolds, and, thus, it is nearly impossible to identify and "score" every component of a lesson. However, what we have attempted to do is provide a guideline to where you could be in terms of your practice. It is extremely hard for us to judge ourselves—some of us are too hard on ourselves, whereas others tend to overreach our levels of achievement. The intent of the matrix is to help you begin to identify what your strengths and weaknesses are and what areas require improvement.

Major Skill Areas

Throughout our research, we have asked the question, "What should be the focal areas that we need to use to ensure good implementation of the SWH strategies?" We have identified four major skill areas. These are:

Dialogical Interactions

Focus of Learning

Connections

Science Argument

Each of these major skill areas has a particular focus that when added together helps teachers to be successful in implementation of the SWH approach and, ultimately, in student learning. Remember, all the skills are interconnected—while we have broken them down into some separate areas, they are distinctly connected. Building strength in one area helps with others; thus, you must build all the areas simultaneously. However, the reverse is not true—concentrating on only one area does not give you strength in the others. Another critical point to remember as you begin the process is that we can concentrate on one or two areas to begin with, and the whole process may appear to be simple. Yet, the more we try the strategies and examine the process, the more complex it becomes. That is not a problem—we just have to remember that it takes time and we have to work at it continually through ongoing reflection and action. We explain each of these skills in greater detail next.

Dialogical Interaction

An absolutely crucial element of the SWH approach is the importance that is placed on negotiation of meaning. Students need to have opportunities to talk with each other in small groups, with their peers as a whole group, and with the teacher. Traditional teaching has centered on the teacher being in charge of the talk—they have structured the types of discussions allowed with emphasis on the teacher being in charge of what is discussed and what knowledge is allowed. This setup has resulted in most questioning being the Initiate, Respond, Evaluate (IRE) pattern, with the teacher at the center controlling the whole process. Shifting to student-centered learning strategies changes this orientation—students construct their own knowledge, and, therefore, we teachers must challenge this knowledge. This requires us to engage the students' knowledge in a public forum. We must use questions that challenge and extend understanding. Most important, we need to listen to students. Dialogue is not a monologue: It requires participants to both talk and listen. Dialogue is about continuing a conversation and thus requires us to interact with the knowledge put forward by others so that the conversation continues to build. For us as teachers, this is often the toughest challenge—to remove ourselves from the center of the conversation. It takes practice. We have provided some examples to explore how this might look across the categories of implementation:

Beginning: Teachers who are in this category are generally doing two things. The first is that all discussion is coming through the teacher. There are very few, or almost no, opportunities for students to initiate a dialogue. The dialogue is controlled by the teacher who is concerned about making sure he is in control of the knowledge being dealt with in the classroom setting. Second, the teacher generally does not ask probing questions, or if she does, she is seeking a single answer. In this stage, we find teachers begin to try asking more open-ended questions. However, they step back from allowing the student voice to be part of the process.

Approaching: Teachers in this category are beginning to ask open-ended questions and try to not evaluate the student responses but fail to follow up with probing questions to explore student thinking. In part, they are beginning to change their questioning strategies and need time to get used to the change. Teachers in this category also attempt to have student-to-student discussion in class, rather than always be the center of attention. However, this is generally not the focus of the talk in the classroom.

Understanding: Teachers in this category are beginning to increase the frequency of student-to-student dialogue in the classroom. They are starting to ask students to explain and challenge each other's responses rather than waiting for the teacher to pass judgment. Teachers use a broad array of questions that begin to probe student understandings and place emphasis on having a conversation with their students with the intention of building understanding, not memorizing the vocabulary of the topic.

Practicing: Teachers in this category are constantly using teacher-student dialogue and student-to-student dialogue to challenge ideas, claims, and evidence. A broad array of questions is used with the intent of developing students' understandings of the topic. While being aware of individual needs, the teacher has an expectation of involvement for all students, with all being required to be part of the dialogue. Student responses are constantly challenged, probed, and extended.

Focus of Learning

In the early chapters of this book, we have focused on who controls learning and how to adopt student-centered strategies. This practice is absolutely critical in terms of promot-

	Level 1 Beginning	Level 2 Approaching	Level 3 Understanding	Level 4 Practicing
Dialogical Interactions	• All discussion coming through the teacher; no or few opportunities for students to initiate a dialogue • Teacher seeks single correct answer, no probing questions • Teacher uses IRE (Initiates, Responds, Evaluates) pattern of questioning	• Teacher attempts student-to-student discussion; provides some opportunities for students to initiate a dialogue • Teacher begins to ask open-ended questions • Teacher begins to use non-evaluative questioning	• Teacher increasing frequency of student-to-student dialogue • Teacher asks many layers of questions (i.e., Bloom's Taxonomy) to begin probing student understanding • Teacher asks students to explain and challenge each other's responses rather than pass judgment • Teachers beginning to place emphasis on having a conversation with the intention of building student understanding	• Teacher constantly using teacher-student dialogue and student-to-student dialogue to challenge ideas, claims, and evidence • Teacher asks many layers of questions (i.e., Bloom's Taxonomy) to build student understanding • Teacher constantly challenges, probes, and extends student responses • Teacher has expectation of all students being involved in the dialogue while being aware of individual needs

Figure 9.3 *Dialogical interaction aspect of the matrix*

ing strategies that enable students to become engaged in learning science and expanding their language use. This requires teachers to change their focus of planning. If learning is about the construction of conceptual frameworks, then teaching has to be oriented toward the "big ideas" or concepts of the topic. This focus on the big idea then needs to be translated into classroom practice. For us the question becomes, how do we continue to focus on helping students engage with the big ideas of the topic? Do we as teachers have a list of content that drives our planning, or do we have a number of big ideas that frame our planning? Is our planning loose enough to deal with unexpected events in class? One of the major problems teachers have is maintaining a focus that encourages students to wrestle with their understandings of the concepts that underpin the topic. When in small groups, students need to have discussions that not only deal with the event or question of the day but also to question how it all fits with the big idea of the topic. The planning needs to build in opportunities for small-group discussions and flexibility not only to move with different student questions/ideas/suggestions about concepts that are not part of the plan but also to move between individual, small-group, and whole-class settings. The difference between teacher-centered and student-centered classrooms is that the focus of learning is not on what the teacher knows and gives to the students, but rather how the teacher constantly strives to engage the students' knowledge and uses this knowledge as the platform for instruction.

Beginning: Teachers in this category tend to plan only for whole-class instruction with the emphasis being on ensuring that they are able to cover the content of the topic. The focus of the SWH is to complete the student template as though it is a worksheet. Students are not provided time to share knowledge and tend to play "guess what is in the teacher's head" games when answering questions.

Approaching: In this category teachers begin to build into their plans some opportunities for students to work in small groups. On some occasions, unexpected results from students are used to add to the lesson, but the emphasis is still on making sure teacher knowledge is the guiding frame of the lesson. The SWH process is moving away from being simply a worksheet. There is some emphasis on ensuring connections are made between claims and evidence and gathering different viewpoints.

Understanding: Teachers in this category regularly plan on using small-group work as a critical component of the lesson, with student knowledge being used within the lesson. There is more comfort with the flexible nature of the SWH process; however, there is still some tension between teacher-centered and student-centered components of knowledge that are dealt with in class. Students are expected to be able to engage in discussions and debates about the topic in framing the arguments that are derived from the inquiry process. Teachers are becoming more comfortable with the degree of flexibility required with the SWH approach.

Practicing: Teachers in this category continually and effectively plan for opportunities for students to be involved in small-group and whole-class work. Teachers are flexible and prepared to move in unanticipated directions; they constantly seek student input and challenge ideas that are brought forward. In this category teachers are very comfortable with the whole SWH approach and are effectively linking the components of questions, claims, evidence, and reflection together.

	Level 1 Beginning	Level 2 Approaching	Level 3 Understanding	Level 4 Practicing
Focus of Learning	• Teacher uses only whole-class grouping for instruction • Focus of SWH is on completion of template • Teacher-centered, teacher-controlled • Little display of confidence in SWH process • No student sharing of knowledge	• Teacher uses whole-class grouping with occasional small groups for instruction • SWH process evident in some connections made between claims and evidence and gathering different viewpoints • Teacher-centered, but occasionally student-centered • Developing confidence in SWH • Some student sharing, but emphasis on teacher knowledge	• Teacher regularly uses a variety of grouping strategies for instruction • SWH process evident in stronger connections between claims and evidence and gathering of different viewpoints • A balance of teacher- and student-centered activities • Shows confidence in flexibility of SWH approach • Students expected to engage in discussions and debates about the topic in framing arguments	• Teacher thoughtfully plans for a variety of appropriate grouping strategies for instruction • SWH process evident in strong connections between claims and evidence, gathering of different viewpoints, and reflections on understanding • Obvious confidence in SWH approach • Students sharing with argumentation with few prompts needed

Figure 9.4 *Focus of learning aspect of the matrix*

Connections

The emphasis of the SWH approach is on the connections that it makes to a range of different areas. Three critical areas of connection are the embedded language practices, the big ideas of the topic, and assessment. The use of language in terms of reading, talking, and writing is absolutely critical in the SWH approach, and, thus, it is important for teachers to constantly make connections to the language components. Examples of these connections include the public debates about each group's claim and evidence to emphasis the scientific argumentation process; the writing of the claims and evidence to ensure that students are making reasoned statements linking these together; the use of different reading sources for determining the validity of claims; and the summary-writing exercise to connect the activities together conceptually. The second area is the connection to the big idea(s) of the unit. As discussed in the early chapters, learning is about the construction of conceptual understanding and the development of conceptual frameworks. To assist this we believe that there is a need for learning to be focused on the conceptual framework. Therefore, teachers must constantly make connections to this organizing frame of the topic, that is, the big ideas. The third area is that of assessment. As teachers we need to move away from multiple-choice questions, fill-in-the-blanks, match-the-words, and short-answer questions. If we are going to involve students in activities that purposefully challenge their ideas and require them to think critically and reason about problems and solutions, we need to assess them in a manner that reflects this approach. Thus we need to use conceptual questions that require students to connect knowledge, explain their understanding, and justify their arguments. These questions need to be about the conceptual framework of the topic, rather than focusing solely on the content points of the topic. Questions must be extended-response-type questions that require and allow students the space to fully answer the questions.

Beginning: Teachers in this category do not make connections to the big ideas of the topic; instead there is only fleeting references to these. Little emphasis is placed on the use of language-based strategies such as diversifying the types of writing used in the classroom, little opportunities for student talk to promote understanding, and reliance on a single information source. Assessment does not reflect the critical thinking and reasoning demands of the approach, but is focused on recall of information.

Approaching: Teachers in this category begin to focus on the big ideas of the topic but tend to do so in a mechanical fashion; that is, they highlight the big ideas but do not use these for building the topic. There is some emphasis on determining student ideas; however, while the teachers seek out these ideas, there is no attempt to build on these ideas. Teachers begin to embed some language practices and place emphasis on student participation in these activities. Assessment is beginning to be focused on challenging students' thinking while still using mostly memory recall items.

Understanding: Teachers in this category connect science to everyday life and build on student knowledge. There is an emphasis on determining student knowledge and building teaching plans based on this knowledge. The big ideas are becoming central to the teaching plan and to the assessment completed by the students. The concept of assessment is better balanced between recall-type questions and extended-response-type questions. Instruction is flexible and uses opportunities for language-based activities to build knowledge.

Practicing: Teachers in this category are consistently using opportunities to connect science with everyday life. They consistently frame their teaching around the big ideas of the topic and promote student learning around these big ideas. Students are constantly required to engage in language practices that promote understanding—for example, diversified writing is undertaken, public debate promotes the function of talk in learning, and multiple sources of information are used to promote reading of a broad range of informational texts. Assessment practices are clearly aligned to the curriculum in using recall- and extended-response-type questions.

Science Argument

The fundamental essence of the SWH approach is the promotion of scientific argument. The scaffolded structure promotes the scientific argument framework of question, claims, evidence, and reflection. Thus, the final focus area is on this critical component.

	Level 1 Beginning	Level 2 Approaching	Level 3 Understanding	Level 4 Practicing
Connections	• Teacher does not make connections to the big ideas of the topic • Science activities do not promote big ideas of the topic • Little emphasis on the use of literacy strategies to promote understanding • Reliance on textbook as single resource • Teacher does not build on or activate students' initial understanding • Assessment does not align with intended and taught curriculum	• Teacher connection to the big ideas of the topic is mechanical • Science activities promote big ideas of the topic in a vague way • Some emphasis on the use of literacy strategies to promote understanding • Beginning use of other resources besides textbook • Teacher moves toward revealing students' initial understanding but fails to use information to make instructional decisions • Assessments might align to curriculum but are recall-focused	• Teacher connection to the big ideas of the topic emphasized • Science activities connected to the big ideas of the topic • Literacy activities used, both planned and unplanned, to promote understanding • Various resources, both print and non-print, used • Teacher works to reveal students' initial understanding and make instructional decisions based on the information • Assessments align to curriculum with a beginning balance of recall and extended-response-type questions	• Teacher consistently frames teaching around big ideas of the topic • Science activities connected to the big ideas of the topic and extend students' learning • Literacy activities, both planned and unplanned, promote and extend understanding • Consistent use of various resources, both print and non-print, used • Teacher effectively reveals students' initial understanding and makes instructional decisions based on the information • Assessments aligned to curriculum with a balance of recall and extended-response-type questions

Figure 9.5 *Connections aspect of the matrix*

The elements that are essential are providing opportunities for students to pose questions, requiring students to construct a concise statement—a claim—as a result of their inquiry and providing reasoned evidence for their claims, and ensuring that they determine how their claims and evidence match up to what is currently known about the topic (reflection). The investigations and argument structures are centered on the big ideas of the topic, and, thus, we believe it is important that the teachers insist that the arguments being constructed by the students are centered on and matched to the big ideas framing the unit study.

Beginning: Teachers in this category are very reluctant to promote student input into the questions for inquiry. Instead they pose the question to be investigated and provide the answers that students are expected to have come up with so that all student answers look exactly the same. There is also a lack of emphasis on student input into the discussion of the data, with little or no attempt made to use the terminology of claims and evidence. As a result students engage very limited use of the scientific argument pattern of question, claims, evidence, and reflection. There is little attempt to build argument connected to the big ideas of the topic.

Approaching: Teachers in this category are beginning to build in opportunities—however limited—for students to pose some questions for the inquiry. The idea of claims and evidence is starting to appear in the teacher dialogue, with some attempt to ensure that the science argument structure is provided to the students. Connections to the big ideas of the topic are made; however, the teacher is providing limited opportunities for the students to debate their thinking in relation to the big ideas.

Understanding: Teachers in this category provide opportunities for students to pose questions and revise them where needed. Students are required to link claims and evidence; that is, students are not allowed to make a claim without providing some form of evidence. The teacher does not consistently scaffold the scientific argument process of question, claims, evidence, and reflection. The big idea of the topic is a central focus of the inquiry, and students are provided some opportunities to debate their ideas in relation to the topic.

Practicing: Teachers in this category provide opportunities for students to pose questions and revise them where needed. Students are consistently required to link claims and evidence, and to use scientific argument where links between question, claims, evidence, and reflection are made. Connections to the big idea of the unit are consistently made and students are required to be involved in debate about these ideas.

How to Use the Matrix

Having outlined the skills and categories for implementation, we now discuss how to use the matrix. A critical point to remember is that it is very difficult for us as individuals to examine our teaching practices by ourselves by just thinking back through the lesson we have just taught. We must make a plan to have opportunities to reflect back on what actually occurred in the lesson. This can be done a number of different ways:

- ❖ Have a colleague sit in your room and make notes. If you do this, we encourage you to have a focus on a particular skill rather than a focus on all the different skills.

- ❖ Videotape the lesson. This is a good way for you to see exactly what you were doing. It may be a little time consuming, but it is an excellent way to have an accurate view of what you are doing.

- ❖ Involve your students in helping you stay on task for a particular skill of questioning, promoting dialogue, or making claims and evidence for example. We have had success when implementing these types of skills by explaining to the students that we have been involved in doing a research project to become a better teacher to help them learn.

	Level 1 Beginning	Level 2 Approaching	Level 3 Understanding	Level 4 Practicing
Science Argument (Questions, Claims, and Evidence)	• Teacher very reluctant to promote student input into the questions for inquiry • Teacher generates the answer to the problem solving • Very limited use of terminology of claims and evidence • Very limited use of scientific argumentation pattern • Little attempt to build argument connected to the big ideas of the topic	• Teacher begins to build limited opportunities for students to pose some questions for the inquiry • Idea of claims and evidence starting to appear in teacher dialogue • Some attempt to ensure science argument structure provided to students • Teacher provides limited opportunities for students to build argument connected to the big ideas of the topic	• Teacher provides opportunities for students to pose questions and some attempt to revise them where needed • Teacher requires students to link claims and evidence • Some scaffolding of instruction provided for the scientific argument process • Big ideas of the topic are the central focus of the inquiry and students are provided some opportunities to debate their ideas	• Teacher provides opportunities for students to pose questions and revise them where needed • Teacher consistently requires students to link claims and evidence • Teacher consistently requires students to use scientific argument where links between question, claims, evidence, and reflection are made • Connections to the big ideas of the unit are consistently made and students are required to be involved in debates about these ideas

Figure 9.6   *Science argumentation aspect of the matrix*

Whatever strategies you use to examine your teaching, you need to understand that time is needed. Improvement in what we do requires practice and reflection.

Teacher's Voice

One thing that I feel would help other teachers embarking on this SWH endeavor would be to start with one unit and to try to find a peer who will join you in making these changes. It has helped me tremendously to have another teacher to discuss ideas with and plan lessons.

While the matrix has been presented as a number of categories and skills, we encourage you to try and focus on one skill in particular as a means to improve all the skills. The skills are interconnected and should be seen as such. However, changing or improving all the skills at one time is a very difficult task. Thus, we suggest some of the following possible strategies:

❖ Plan to use the basic structure of the SWH; that is, plan to make sure the concept of question, claims, evidence, and reflection are built in to your lesson.

❖ Choose one of the skills, for example, dialogical interaction, and try to define what you think your strengths and weaknesses are with this skill.

❖ Prepare a few cues that you could use to practice the skill, for example, try not to confirm a student's answer. Rather, ask another student, ask students for clarification of their answer, and try to move away from "guess what is in my head" games.

❖ Plan a process that allows for monitoring of your skill.

❖ Try to organize a colleague who you can work with to review the analysis of the lesson.

❖ Plan for the next practice session. Changing skills is a tough task and requires continued practice.

❖ As you get better at one skill, begin to examine how this skill meshes with another skill in the matrix.

We cannot stress enough that we need to remove ourselves from the center of the action. The greatest turning point for teachers that we have found is when they stop talking, get out of the way, and let the students do the thinking. The skills outlined are about making student-centered learning environments the focus of our teaching.

Do not be discouraged when everything does not go as planned or if things quickly become too complicated. We are dealing with real human beings, not robots. Raise the bar on your level of expectation for yourself and your students, and you will find that change will take place in your classroom.

Teacher's Voice

First-Grade Teacher: As a teacher, I have had many aha moments through learning about the SWH approach. I feel like this process is like an onion and I am getting caught up in the fine details of the layers. I need to remember that the "big idea" is the onion itself as a whole. I need to back up and remember to look at the whole onion often—then I can return to the layers and explore and analyze each tiny layer, always remembering to back up often and take a big look again.

Third-Grade Teacher: My aha moment came when I realized that I did not need to follow the SWH "template" in lock-step fashion. We could interweave the claim, research, and evidence pieces as the need arose. It was OK to change the question or to revise after doing perhaps yet another SWH discovery.

Examples of Implementation

Next we have tried to provide two case studies of implementation that we hope will help you understand some of the challenges that we as teachers face in using these approaches. We would like to re-emphasize that there is no single pathway to success—we will all have different ways that we do things. However, we do know that constantly striving to challenge students' thinking and requiring science argument is critical in promoting understanding of the science concepts. The case studies described next are constructed from a number of different studies that we have been involved with and do not reflect any one teacher.

Case Study 1

Betty is an experienced fifth-grade teacher who has been using the SWH approach for two years. She has been using the student template as the report format for her students. The students are required to complete all sections of the template, and her marking scheme has equal points allocated for each section of the template. She is still struggling with her questioning skills—at times she begins to try to pass student answers back to the group but too often steps back and seeks to play "guess what is in my head" games. She appears to lack confidence in students' abilities to think deeply and thus does not relax enough to give them opportunities to demonstrate that they can. This creates a catch-22 situation. Because she does not completely trust the students to address all the conceptual knowledge, she places emphasis on ensuring that *she* covers all the content knowledge. Thus Betty struggles with balancing the coverage of content knowledge with the big ideas of the topic, so she also finds it difficult to focus learning on the big ideas of the topic. When she begins to let students have some space in terms of discussing the ideas from the inquiry activities, she gets excited by what they are saying but struggles to move forward in using the students' ideas. In terms of planning for these activities, she has not done enough forward planning in relation to constructing a concept map of the topic, and thus is very concerned when students take the conversation away from her direction for the unit. We would say that Betty is in the Beginning stage but moving toward the Approaching stage.

Case Study 2

Judy is an experienced second-grade teacher who has been using the SWH approach for three years. During this time she has continued to improve her skills and has worked hard to be more student-centered in her use of the SWH approach. Her questioning of students is consistently focused on trying to explore students' understandings, where she ensures that students are constantly challenged when providing answers. Students are challenged to provide supporting evidence when making a claim both when talking about their activities and when writing up their SWH reports. At the completion of activities, each small group is required to present their claims and evidence to the class. They are expected to explain their reasoning for their claim, and the class as a whole explores consensus for a whole-class-constructed claim. Judy struggles at times to link the science activities with some of the language activities that could strengthen student understanding. While she requires her students to use many types of writing to summarize their learning in the unit, she does not consistently give students enough writing time to truly negotiate meaning. She is beginning to make better use of her concept map planning for the unit; she is now much more comfortable in allowing students to move along pathways that are not always productive in building knowledge. Having constructed the concept map she is now confident in being able to redirect students through her questioning strategies. We would say that Judy is in the Understanding phase moving into the Practicing stage.

Key Understandings

Remember, in trying to construct your own rating be realistic and fair to yourself. Change takes time and you need to keep practicing and view your own teaching practice.

CHAPTER 10

Frequently Asked Questions and Benefits of This Approach

In this chapter we present some frequently asked questions for the reader. These questions were generated and answered by the thirty-two teachers who have been a part of our elementary SWH study for the past three years. The teachers were asked to put together some questions that they believed were ones that they wanted to know about when they started implementing the SWH in their own classrooms. While there are many possible questions, we kept the total to eleven. Thus, they are more general in nature, but we believe that they do answer some of the initial concerns of teachers.

We wanted to present to the reader some results that we have gathered in our research into using the SWH approach. We have been fortunate to work with a number of schools and their teachers, and to be able to explore what we believe are some critical questions about the benefits and difficulties that arise when using the SWH approach. While we present some general benefits, a list of the research articles and conference presentations that we have been involved with is provided for further reading and investigation.

Frequently Asked Questions

As we described previously, the intent of this section is to provide the reader with some questions and answers from teachers who have used the SWH for a number of years. Thus the questions and answers are based in real experience and not on the imagination of the authors.

Why Would You Use SWH?

SWH allows students to be in charge of their own learning. You start with what students know and build on that knowledge. Students generate the questions that provide the framework for the unit of study. SWH provides opportunities for inquiry-based hands-on science experiences and multiple language experiences. It gives students a purpose for reading and writing.

How Does Use of SWH Impact/Reach Students with Special Needs?

I have found in my classroom that students with special needs do very well with this approach. Since we focus on conceptual learning and not "picky little details," I find they can have success. The inquiry-based approach meets their needs along with the varied nonfiction print used during this unit. I adapt for their lower reading and writing skills by doing pair reading, using leveled nonfiction books, employing partner and group work, and using a resource teacher at times to help and provide additional support.

How Do You Incorporate Grading with SWH?

Teacher #1—Grade Three

To begin with, in third grade, we do much of the SWH template together to model the process. We work on science content as well as our language skills such as capitalization, punctuation, and writing in complete sentences. Because the template is done together in many of the first units, no grade is taken on science content, but a language grade is taken for the question and test area of the template.

Eventually, more responsibility is given to students to fill out the template on their own. Then, the question, test, claims, and evidence areas are graded for language and science content, usually on a scale of one to five. I don't typically score the rest of the template.

Other pieces of work that I grade include writing samples, such as quick writes, journal entries regarding what we have been doing in science, and the final writing projects. The quick writes and journal entries are also scored on a scale of one to five, both for language skills and science content. The final project is worth more points, because it is longer and more involved.

Pretests are scored and recorded but not graded. Posttests are scored, recorded, and graded. For a final unit grade, I also take into account improvement between pre- and posttest scores. Discussion throughout the unit is also taken into account for a final grade. Grading can be somewhat subjective, but the use of the rating scale and the multiple data points I am looking at help me to determine the student's grade.

Teacher #2—Grade Five

There are several opportunities throughout an SWH unit to take grades. The hardest part as a teacher is determining how to grade each item and what to look for. Sometimes I grade for science content, sometimes I grade for language components, while other times I grade for both.

This year I decided not to grade the posttest. Instead, I looked at the growth that was made from the pre- to posttest and showed this data to the students.

One item I grade is the SWH template for each investigation. As the fifth-grade teacher, I have the advantage of having the second- and third-grade teachers using the same process, and, therefore, they are familiar with the template. After a few times of doing templates together, students are off on their own.

I grade each component of the template. I've even had students take the template and write each section in paragraph form. In this way, I feel more comfortable grading for the language components.

I also use various graphic organizers throughout the unit. I always grade these for science content, but they could easily be graded for language components as well.

At the end of each unit students do a final writing project. I grade this for both science content and language components.

Teacher #3—Kindergarten

For pre- and posttests, I audiotape answers to conceptual questions. We also make observations of students during "exploring" time and write anecdotal records about their learning. Another data source comes from taking pictures of their explorations. For example, the students sort animals and then do it again at the end and see if their sorting is the same or different. Make sure the students are in the picture! It is also possible to create a pre- and posttest checklist for the teacher to fill out or a rubric for teachers to record conceptual questions.

Teacher #4—Grade Three

We create a rubric for the SWH process. An example includes the following categories: working in a group, writing/ language piece, understanding vocabulary, and demonstrating the science concept. (For an example of a rubric, see Chapter 8.)

How Much Time Do I Spend on a Unit?

My units vary in length. Some have lasted up to three or four months, others take between one and two months. The length of my units depends on a few things: time, student interest, and content. After I develop my big ideas—the basic information I need to teach based on the district's standards and benchmarks—I depend on the students' questions to drive my lessons. On a daily basis, in my sixth-grade classroom, we typically spend between an hour and an hour and a half, depending on the topic.

Where Do I Start?

To start my units, I pinpoint my big ideas and create a pre- and posttest to assess the students' learning. We start our units by creating a classroom concept map on the board. Then I have students make their own. After concept maps, I have students develop questions that they have, possibly on their own or in groups. Next I take their questions and concept maps and look at them to see where they are and where they need to start. Our projects and lessons are built from their questions. I also allow them to ask questions throughout our unit to continuously inquire about our topics. From there, I try to set some type of time line to manage my time so that I can include the units I need to do in the year (based on my standards and benchmarks).

How Do I Justify the Amount of Time It Takes to Do a Unit?

The SWH process does take time, but we feel it is time well spent. In takes time for students to negotiate meaning about the concepts we are teaching. We have learned not to worry about "covering the book"; it is far more important to focus on the standards and dig deep into concepts. In this process, we continually work to help students learn conceptually. Language arts is integrated with science in the SWH process as students read, write, and think conceptually about science content. Students are exposed to nonfiction materials, which motivate them to learn and are engaging and interesting.

How Do I Integrate SWH with My State Standards?

I identify each standard and benchmark that I am responsible for covering at my grade level. I pull a big idea from each of these benchmarks to begin my unit. This big idea guides my development of the conceptual questions on my pre- and posttest. As I proceed through the unit, I constantly refer back to the big idea, which in turn links back to my state and district standards.

Where Do I Find Print Resources Needed for My Unit?

We are fortunate in Iowa to have a wide variety of print resources and kits available through our Area Education Agencies. We use the AEA library for nonfiction books and films as well as science kits to supplement our units. In addition, we use the school library as well as the public libraries in our communities to supplement our classroom collection as we study concepts and topics. We use the United Streaming website, www.unitedstreaming.com, for video clips to augment our units. Teachers and students engage in online research to look for answers to questions. We use our textbooks, but as resources, reading from specific pages that support our science standards and benchmarks.

What Do You Do with the Students Who Are Absent?

We know that in order for students to learn they have to engage in and negotiate understanding. Students are in charge of their learning, and as they negotiate their understanding, they need to be present at school to experience and discuss the science content. However, absences are unavoidable. Here are some of the varied ways that teachers in our project handle absences:

- ❖ The student completes the science lab at recess. (Interestingly enough, students don't usually complain about this, because they enjoy the science experiences!)
- ❖ Students who were in class discuss and explain what happened in the lab experience to those who were absent.
- ❖ The teacher performs a mini-demonstration: Students who are there demonstrate for students who were absent.
- ❖ Sometimes, students are simply "excused" from that activity.
- ❖ Sometimes, we can't recreate the activity itself, so students read the content or read about a similar lab experience or experiment.
- ❖ The student reads an article and writes a summary or questions.
- ❖ Discussions carry over, so if a student misses one day, he can get the gist of the activity.

When Do You Introduce the Big Idea?

Response #1

On the plant unit I laid out materials for the students to make a plant. When we came back in a big group they had to explain their plant to class. After that we talked about some common things seen in the plants. The students came up with their own big idea: Plants have common parts. Later, after other experiments and discussions, we changed things to features and added all plants.

Response #2

It depends on what your big idea is and the knowledge students bring into your unit. For instance, in a fourth-grade unit on electricity, if your big idea is "electrical circuits require a complete loop through which an electrical current may pass," you would want to wait until the students discover it for themselves. Another example in a fourth-grade unit when you might wait would be a big idea about the solar system that states "the moon moves across the sky on a daily basis much like the sun." After many activities and research, students will begin to gain understanding of this big idea. We will not always introduce them later. In a preschool unit about animal needs, the big idea "animals have basic needs to survive" could be introduced at the beginning of the unit. Simply stating this big idea does not give away any answers. You will provide activities throughout the unit that consistently connect to the big idea. Just know yourself as the teacher and understand that there is no set time required to introduce the big idea.

Response #3

The teacher can use a concept map or children's books at the beginning. Sometimes through discussion the kids will generate a big idea.

What Do You Do When a Child Refuses to Give Up an Inaccurate Claim?

Teacher Response #1

Do more research. Do another activity that might help those students clarify their claim. Hold a class discussion and have peers share and as a class discover a claim because students listen to peers! If they all have the same misconception plan another activity.

Teacher Response #2

Ask the students to research or lead them to further investigate the claim to find more evidence. By working in groups, the students can together to find more information.

Benefits of the SWH Approach

We have been involved in researching the implementation of the SWH approach for the last eight years. During this time we have students in preschool classrooms through freshman chemistry students at a university using this approach. A number of clear benefits have been achieved when using this approach. However, the benefits depend upon the quality of the implementation. We cannot stress this enough. The SWH approach is a combination of teacher quality and embedded-language-based science inquiry experiences. One by itself will not lead to the same result as the combination of the two. Embedded-language practices, scientific argumentation, or teacher implementation alone will not give the same benefits as integrating all of these together.

In discussing the benefits, we point out that the results indicated have all been statistically significant, and papers reporting these are listed at the end of this chapter.

Our studies have attempted to measure the difference between high- and low-quality implementation of the SWH approach to determine what students think about using the strategies, and how several school districts have responded to its teachers using the approach. The benefits include:

1. Closing the achievement gap. The SWH approach has been successful in closing the gap between low achievers and high achievers. This has occurred with students at the elementary, middle school, high school, and university level. The gap is not closed but is significantly reduced. High-achieving students' scores have remained the same while the low-achieving students' scores are increased. In some cases we have half the gap between the pre- and posttest measures. In other studies, the gap has been almost closed, while in one study with tenth-grade students we have the low-achieving students outperforming the high-achieving students.

2. Closing the gender gap. Much attention has been focused on the disparity between genders in relation to science teaching in school. We have shown that we have been able to close this gap when students are engaged with the SWH approach. The low-achieving males are successful using this approach, not just females.

3. Performance on Iowa Test of Basic Skills. With the school districts that we have been working with for three consecutive years, their scores on the less-proficient level have fallen from the low 30 percent range to the high teens percent range. This takes into account a range of teacher implementation levels. These students have moved into the proficient range, with the percentage of students at above proficient remaining relatively constant.

4. Benefits for students with Individual Educational Programs (IEP students). The interesting benefits seen with this group of students is that while raw scores are lower than non-IEP students, their rate of improvement in science is greater than the non-IEP students with high-quality implementation. These students become more engaged and tend to improve their conceptual understandings in a richer way than when using more traditional approaches.

5. Benefits for low socioeconomic status (SES) students. As with the IEP students, we have seen gains made by the low-SES students to close the gap between low-SES and higher-SES students. In a study with grades four, five, and six, low-SES students with high levels of implementation outperformed the higher-SES students.

While these results point to the benefits gained in terms of statistical data, we have conducted interviews with students over a number of years. From these interviews we can also note a number of clear benefits that students believe arise from being involved with the SWH approach. These include:

1. A greater control over the activity leads to more involvement in the activity. Students consistently point to the ability to pose questions and have some control over the direction of the activity leading to a much greater sense of having some control of what they are able to do. This not only applies to the actual activity but also to their willingness to be involved in the discussion and debates.

2. Students believe that they are learning when they use the SWH approach. Students indicate that having to make claims and provide evidence, and having to compare their answers with others have a very positive outcome for them in terms of their learning. They believe that as a consequence of the question structure they are involved with that they begin to understand the big ideas of the topic.

3. Students believe that they are more confident in answering test questions. When asked about how confident they feel about answering test questions, the students have consistently told us that they feel more confident than when using traditional lab reports. Even though little time is spent on answering end-of-chapter questions, they feel that with the big ideas and discussions in class, they are confident about doing well on the test.

In summary, we remind the reader that we believe the SWH approach does have benefits for both teachers and students. However, these benefits vary and might take time to materialize. We can say that the better we as teachers implement the SWH approach, the richer the benefits are for the students and their learning.

Research Papers and Presentations for Further Reading

(Also, visit our website for a complete list of publications and presentations as well as links to a variety of papers and multimedia presentations.)

Website Address: http://www.ci.hs.iastate.edu/scilit

Burke, Kathy, Jason Poock, Thomas Greenbowe, and Brian Hand. 2005. Training chemistry teaching assistants to use the science writing heuristic. *Journal of College Science Teaching*, 35 (1), 36–41.

Greenbowe, Thomas J., and Brian Hand. 2005. Introduction to the Science Writing Heuristic. In Norbert J. Pienta, Melanie M. Cooper, and Thomas J. Greenbowe (Eds.). *Chemists' Guide to Effective Teaching*. Upper Saddle River, NJ: Prentice Hall.

Hand, Brian (Ed.). 2008. *Science Inquiry, Argument and Language: A Case for the Science Writing Heuristic.* Rotterdam: Sense Publishers.

Hand, Brian, Liesl Hohenshell, and Vaughn Prain. 2004. Exploring students' responses to conceptual questions when engaged with planned writing experiences: a study with year 10 science students. *Journal of Research in Science Teaching, 41*, 186–210.

Hand, Brian, Carolyn Wallace, and Eun-Mi Yang. 2004. Using the science writing heuristic to enhance learning outcomes from laboratory activities in seventh grade science: Quantitative and qualitative aspects. *International Journal of Science Education*, 26, 131–49.

Hohenshell, Liesl, and Brian Hand. 2006. Writing-to-learn strategies in secondary school cell biology. *International Journal of Science Education*, 28, 261–89.

Rudd, James A., Thomas J. Greenbowe, and Brian Hand. 2001. Reshaping the general chemistry laboratory report using the science writing heuristic. *Journal of College Science Teaching, 31,* 230–34.

Rudd, James A., Thomas J. Greenbowe, Brian Hand, and M. L. Legg. 2001. Using the Science Writing Heuristic to move toward an inquiry-based laboratory curriculum: An example from physical equilibrium. *Journal of Chemical Education, 78,* 1680–86.

Wallace, Carolyn, Brian Hand, and Vaughn Prain. 2004. *Writing and Learning in the Science Classroom.* Boston: Kluwer Press.

Wallace, Carolyn, Brian Hand, and Eun-Mi Yang. 2004. The Science Writing Heuristic: Using writing as a tool for learning in the laboratory. In E. Wendy Saul (Ed.). *Border Crossing: Essays on Literacy and Science.* Newark, DE: International Reading Association.

Afterword—One Final Claim

Denny Taylor once said, "There is never a time when I pull my chair alongside a child and a miracle doesn't appear" (quoted in Calkins 2001, p. 10). For the past several years, we have had the opportunity to do just that— pull our chairs up next to children who shared stories, thinking, questions, claims, and evidence. Seven hundred children each year engaged in the Science Writing Heuristic from different places and spaces (rural, urban, suburban), at different ages (four to thirteen years old), and in different grades (preschool through grade six). Some of the students live in isolated rural areas and others in bustling metropolises. Some are English language learners. Some live in poverty. Others live with the realities of incarceration, war, cancer, and other of life's challenges.

Our final claim is that this book is richer (a real "page turner") because children were willing to share their stories. We could not include all the writing samples and stories (six file cabinets full!), but the ones here represent the collective work of many students, families, and teachers. Calkins (2001) states, "Teaching begins with seeing the significance and intelligence of what children are doing—and almost doing" (p. 10). That is our final wish for you: Have a go with this approach, pull your chair up alongside a child, and watch the miracles appear.

Have A Go!—Appendix Overview

Getting started with a new approach can be a pretty daunting task. One of the suggestions that emerged when teachers read the first draft of this text was this: Can you break it up into some small, easy steps to help us get started? This appendix is our response with a resounding, "Yes!" As you work through each of the chapters, we have encouraged you in different places in the text to "have a go!" and find your way to these small challenges in the back of the book. "Have a go" is often a term that we use to tell young writers when they are struggling with the spelling of a new word. We ask them to "have a go" with it, give it a try, see what happens! Just as we would pose this challenge to young writers, we encourage you to have a go with the SWH and *S*ee *W*hat *H*appens!

Appendix A: What Do I Know About Myself as a Learner?

Appendix B: What Do I Know About the Big Idea(s)?
What Should My Students Know About the Big Idea(s)?

Appendix C: How Do I Know What My Students Know About the Big Idea(s)?

Appendix D: How Do I Question the Students?

Appendix E: How Do I Help Students with Claims and Evidence?

Appendix F: How Do I Get Students to Negotiate Their Understanding?

Appendix G: How Do I Incorporate Literature into My SWH Units?

What Do I Know About Myself as a Learner?

What do we know about ourselves as learners? When was the last time that we sat down and thought about the conditions that we require for ourselves as learners—not as teachers but as adults learning something new?

Try completing the following task: Write down something that you would consider yourself an expert at. On the flip side, write down something you are terrible at, in other words, something you don't do well at all. Return to the side of the paper where your expert task is written. Now, write down the five ways you became an expert at this task, skill, or the like. See if your answers match these common responses:

❖ Have time to explore on my own

❖ Given opportunities to ask experts

❖ Have the right equipment available to use

❖ Have interest in the topic

❖ Provided opportunities to practice

❖ Controlled the pace of learning

These responses seem to be straightforward and reasonable. Now go to the flip side—make a short list of why you struggle so much with this task that you don't do well at all. Many times, the responses are:

❖ Don't have interest in learning

❖ Was told exactly what to do or forced to do it

❖ Have no skill at doing it

❖ Answer questions out of the text or rote learning

❖ Take the experts' ideas or strategies word for word or step by step

The question is, why do we not put the learning strategies that are most effective for ourselves as learners into our classrooms? Of course, one of the first responses to that question is, "Yeah, but we have to . . ." Here are two interesting points to ponder:

❖ First, why is it that when someone talks to a group of people, or shows a group of people a new skill, that no two people in the groups repeat the message or skill in exactly the same manner as the person who was in charge?

❖ Second, why is it that all students are not succeeding equally well if the current strategies implemented mean that as teachers we control the information they receive?

Your understanding of teaching and learning is fundamental to teaching with questions, claims, and evidence. Continue to reflect back on this exercise as you implement in the classroom.

What Do I Know About the Big Idea(s)? What Should My Students Know About the Big Idea(s)?

There are many documents to help you determine the big idea for your unit. First, you should consult your district or state's standards and benchmarks documents for science and literacy. Literacy standards and benchmarks can support your big idea of science. Other resources that might help you articulate the big idea(s) for your unit are described in the following sections.

Science

American Association for the Advancement of Science. 1993. *Benchmarks for Science Literacy*. New York: Oxford University Press.

American Association for the Advancement of Science. 2001. *Atlas of Science Literacy*. Washington, D.C.: American Association for the Advance of Science and National Science Teachers Association.

National Research Council. 1995. *National Science Education Standards*. Washington, D.C.: National Academy Press.

Tetley, Juliana, and Ann L. Wild. 1998. *NSTA Pathways to the Science Standards*. Washington, D.C.: National Academy Press.

United States Department of Education. 2006. *Science Framework for the 2009 National Assessment of Educational Progress Prepublication Edition*. Washington, D.C.: National Assessment Governing Board.

Literacy

Hillocks, George. 1987. May. Synthesis of research on teaching writing. *Educational Leadership, 44*(8), 71–82.

Learning Research Development Center. 2004. *New Standards: Reading and Writing Grade by Grade*. Washington, D.C.: National Center on Education and the Economy.

United States Department of Education. 1997. *Writing Framework and Specifications for the 1998 National Assessment of Educational Progress*. Washington, D.C.: National Assessment Governing Board.

United States Department of Education. 2005. *Reading Framework for the 2009 National Assessment of Educational Progress*, pre-publication edition. Washington, D.C. National Assessment Governing Board.

Also, a helpful website in examining the big ideas in literacy is the cooperative project between the National Council of Teachers of English and the International Reading Association, which can be found at www.readwritethink.org. Figure B.1 shows examples of science benchmarks and aligned big ideas developed by K–8 teachers implementing the SWH approach.

Benchmark	Big Idea
• Understand plants and animals progress through sequential stages that include beginning, growth, development, and and reproduction	• All living things complete a life cycle
• Understand different types of plants and animals have different life-cycle stages, but the stages might be similar for similar kinds of plants and animals	
• Light, heat, electricity, and magnetism	• Electricity in circuits can produce light, heat, sound, and magnetic effects
	• Electrical circuits require a complete loop through which an electrical current can pass
• Students demonstrate an understanding of properties of objects and materials	• Materials can exist in different states—solid, liquid, and gas
	• Some materials can be changed from one state to another by heating and cooling
• Students demonstrate an understanding of organisms and environments	• All animals depend on plants • Some animals eat plants for food
	• Other animals eat animals that eat the plants
• Properties of objects and materials • Light, heat, electricity, and magnetism	• Objects can be described by their properties and the materials they are made from
• Objects have many observable properties	• Objects (things) have properties (stuff) that you can see and feel
• Know the integral parts and functions of systems	• The human body has systems that interact with each other
• Know that materials can change from solid to liquid to gas by heating and from gas to liquid to solid by cooling	• Materials can exist in different states—solid, liquid, and gas
• Organisms have basic needs • Plants have parts or structures that help them live in different places	• All plants have specific needs and parts (structures) that help them grow in different places
• Know that animals have features that help them live in different environments • Know that animals closely resemble their parents • Know that animals require air, water, food, and shelter	• Animals have body parts to help them live • Animals look like their parents • Animals need things to live
• Understand and apply knowledge of structure and function in living systems	• The structure and function of living systems are essential for life processes
• Understand and apply knowledge of the earth system • Water cycle	• Water on Earth goes through a cycle

Benchmark	Big Idea
• Understand how a combination of constructive and destructive weathering and erosion forces create landforms	• Mass movement can be constructive and destructive in the creation of new landforms
• Understand and apply knowledge of changes in the earth and sky • Weather changes • Describing weather	• Weather changes from day to day and over the seasons • Weather can be described by measurable quantities such as temperature, wind direction and speed, and precipitation
• Understand and apply knowledge of properties and changes in properties in matter (standard)	• The world operates by motions and forces
• Plants and animals have features that enable them to survive in various environmental conditions	• Living things interact with and depend upon one another and their environment

Figure B.1 *Benchmarks and big ideas*

What Should My Kids Know About the Big Idea(s)?

Again, your standards and benchmarks document is the first resource to reference when you are trying to determine what your students need to know. Also, refer to the resources listed in the previous section to further define what is developmentally appropriate for the age of your students.

What Do I Know About the Big Idea(s): Creating Your First Concept Map

Thinking about a topic conceptually is different from normal practice and, thus, is more difficult. It does take some time. The concepts are not laid out very well in the textbooks. How strong is my (the teacher) understanding of the topic? How easy would it be for me to draw a concept map of the topic? Let's try it! (You might want to pick a topic you are very familiar with before doing this exercise with your big idea from science.)

Materials

❖ Large, blank piece of paper or whiteboard

❖ Sticky notes

❖ Marker or pen

Step 1: What is the big idea of your unit? What is the major idea(s) that students will take with them, no matter where they are, and be able to use it?

Step 2: Write this idea in the center of your paper. (There are many types of concept maps—only one is described here.)

Step 3: Brainstorm words and phrases that relate to your topic. Write each word or phrase onto a separate sticky note.

Step 4: Reread each sticky note, categorizing them into clusters or groups that make sense to you.

Step 5: Place them in categories around your big idea.

Step 6: Draw arrows out from your big idea to each group.

Step 7: Draw arrows from group to group showing your understanding of any connections/relationships.

Step 8: Write words/phrases on each arrow to link one thought to another—and the big idea to your groups.

Step 9: "Read" your concept map. Does it show your understanding of the big idea? Can you explain your thinking through the use of this concept map?

It might have been harder than you thought to do a concept map! What from your experience can you transfer to the classroom? Following is one example of a teacher's first concept map. She used the computer program Inspiration/Kidspiration to create her map.

Figure B.2 *Teacher concept map*

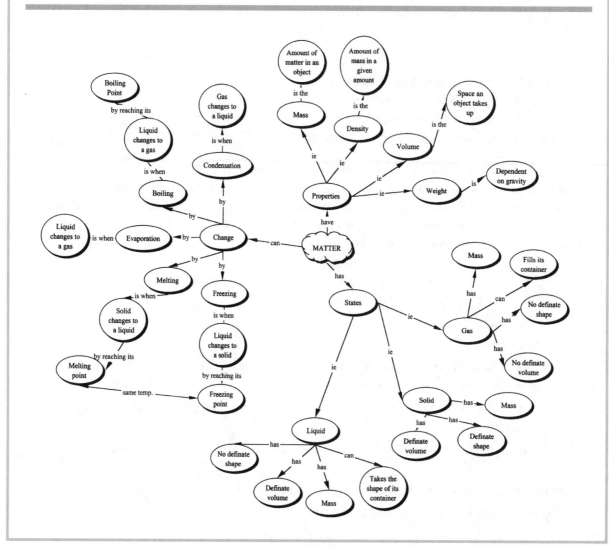

How Do I Know What My Students Know About the Big Idea(s)?

Research is clear that for students to learn, they must first be aware of their current understanding. There are many ways to activate prior knowledge while determining what kids know in order to inform instruction. You can read more about these strategies in Chapters 5 and 8.

Concept Maps

The steps we use in developing a concept map follow:

- ❖ Write the topic to be studied—the big idea—on a large piece of paper, the whiteboard, or the chalkboard. The map should be in a large enough area that students will be able to see it, preferably in an area where the map can be left to add to as new understandings and negotiations are made.
    - ❖ The topic can be placed in the middle, on the top, on the side, or on the bottom of the map.
- ❖ Give students sticky notes. Instruct students to think about what they know about the topic by brainstorming.
    - ❖ On each sticky note students write one word or phrase about the topic.
    - ❖ Students write their initials or names on each sticky note they write.
- ❖ After students have time to brainstorm, students bring their sticky notes up to the board and read them to the class.
    - ❖ Sticky notes containing the same phrase or key word are placed on top of one another.
- ❖ The teacher and the students work together to group or classify similar ideas into categories.
- ❖ Linking words are added to the map to connect the concept to the categories so that anyone who looks at the map can see how each item is related.
- ❖ As the students negotiate new understandings, additional sticky notes are added. These sticky notes are generally a different color than the first notes placed on the map.

Primary teachers might find the following modifications useful in developing the concept map:

- ❖ As students brainstorm, the teacher can record each thought and/or draw a picture on 8½ × 11 paper instead of using a sticky note.
- ❖ After the brainstorming session, the teacher and the class work together to group the ideas into categories. This categorization can be done on the board or on the floor. One possible way to help students visualize this process is to use yarn and place it around the categories once they are established.
- ❖ Yarn can also be used to link the concept to the categories of words. Tape or staple the linking word on top of the yarn. Linking words, which help everyone see how the categories relate to the topic, can be as simple as *are*, *makes*, or *have*.

Posting the concept map in a prominent place in the classroom helps to keep the class focused on the learning and the big ideas. Students enjoy adding to the concept map and changing it as they develop and negotiate new understandings. See some examples of student concept maps in Chapter 3. Various other graphic organizers that can also help you gain insight into what your students know about the big idea before you begin a unit can be found in Figure C.1.

Classroom Discussions and Paying Attention

Something that teachers do every day is ask students to discuss a variety of topics across the curriculum. As students are discussing, teachers can watch kids and listen, paying attention to their developing understandings (and misconceptions). It is amazing what one can discover by being a silent observer in the classroom, watching and listening to what students are talking about related to the topic at hand. Use a clipboard and walk around your classroom as students are discussing. Write down what you hear students talking about. Resist the temptation at this point to comment on students' current understandings. Simply record their comments.

Topics of discussion should be aligned to your big idea but can come from many places including current events, textbooks, read alouds, video clips, PWIM posters, and the like.

Figure C.1a *Graphic organizer to get started with prior knowledge*

Know-Wonder-Learn

Question:

Know	Wonder	Learn

How My Ideas Change

Big Idea or Question to Be Investigated	My Beginning Understanding	My New Understanding

Topic/Big Idea	Evidence of Understanding/ Lack of Understanding/ Misconceptions Date: _____	Evidence of Understanding/ Lack of Understanding/ Misconceptions Date: _____

How Do I Question the Students?

Some suggestions for examining questioning in your own teaching:

❖ Write down some questions about the topic you will be teaching tomorrow. Avoid questions that are "Guess what is in my head"—stick to questions that will make students think. It takes time to move away from what we have always used.

❖ Look at the questions you generated earlier. Where do they fall on Bloom's Taxonomy (see Figure D.1)? Can you move the questions to a higher level? It is important to have questions at various levels. Knowledge-level questions are essential for building a foundation for understanding, but students need to be pushed to critical-thinking levels.

❖ To begin changing your questioning strategies, tell the students that today you are trying something new and you are not allowed to give answers to questions. Every time you ask a question, ask another student to comment.

    ❖ For example, "Mary, what do you think about what Carmen said? Why?"

❖ What if the students agree to an answer and it is wrong? Then you as the teacher need to pose a question that will challenge the answer. For example, you might comment, "I like the answer you put forward about X, but I was wondering what would happen if I did Y?" Remember, simply telling the answer has not worked in the past—changes to ideas occur because the students make the change, not the teacher.

❖ Give the students time to talk through possible answers with their peers. For example, "Turn to your partner and decide on your answer and a reason for your answer. You have two minutes." Then you can seek the groups that have the same answer or different answers and ask them to explain their reasoning.

Negotiating meaning is *not* about passing on information; it is about challenging students to account for their ideas and maneuver them toward scientifically acceptable ideas. One way to get started is—just as a teacher suggested in the introduction to Section III—simply begin by asking "Why?" to everything. Never answer, always question!

Figure D.1 *Working with Bloom's Taxonomy*

Level	Description	A Question . . .
Level 1 Knowledge	These are questions that check the basic facts about people, places, or things.	
Level 2 Comprehension	These are questions that check your understanding and memory of facts.	
Level 3 Application	These questions test your ability to use your knowledge in a problem-solving, practical manner.	
Level 4 Analysis	These are questions in which we select, examine, and break apart information into its smaller, separate parts.	
Level 5 Synthesis	These questions are those in which you utilize the basic information in a new, original, or unique way.	
Level 6 Evaluation	These are questions that help us decide on the value of our information. They enable us to make judgments about the information.	

How Do I Help Students with Claims and Evidence?

Many teachers have used the following story, "Mr. Xavier," developed by James Rudd to help students understand the importance of evidence. (A great way to model fluent reading for students is for the teacher to read this story aloud to hold the attention of and engage *all* students.) See more student examples using this story in Chapter 6 and 7.

Mr. Xavier

You and your partner are private detectives who have been hired to investigate the death of the wealthy but eccentric Mr. Xavier, a man who was well known for his riches and his reclusive nature. He avoided being around others because he was always filled with anxiety and startled easily. He also suffered from paranoia, and he would fire servants who he had employed for a long time because he feared they were secretly plotting against him. He would also eat the same meal for dinner every night, two steaks cooked rare and two baked potatoes with sour cream.

Upon arriving at the tragic scene, you are told that Mr. Xavier was found dead in his home early this morning by the servants. The previous evening after the chef had prepared the usual dinner for Mr. Xavier, the servants had been dismissed early in order to avoid returning home during last night's terrible storm. When they returned in the morning, Mr. Xavier's body was found facedown in the dining room.

Looking into the room, you start your investigation. The large window in the dining room has been shattered and appears to have been smashed open from the outside. The body exhibits laceration wounds and lies facedown by the table, and there is a large red stain on the carpet that emanates from under the body. An open bottle of red wine and a partially eaten steak still remain on the table. A chair that has been tipped over is next to the body, and under the table is a knife with blood on it.

After the students have read the story, engage them in the following discussion: *Based on these preliminary observations, please work with your partner to draw initial conclusions about what happened. Please provide as much evidence as you can to support each conclusion you make.*

Take a moment and follow the directions given in the Mr. Xavier story. What claims can you make? What is your evidence? How will this activity help students develop an understanding of the importance of evidence in a scientific investigation? Primary-grade teachers may wish to provide an alternate form of this story.

Another way to experience claims and evidence is to practice using familiar content such as the following activity using song titles:

❖ In the next thirty seconds, think of a song title that symbolizes your feelings toward the SWH. At the end of the thirty seconds, state the title and the rationale for your choice (claim and evidence).

❖ Now use the following graphic organizer and think of as many song titles as you can in thirty seconds.

❖ Were you able to think of more examples than the first attempt? How would you compare the ease of the two attempts?

❖ If you were asked to write a paragraph, including song title possibilities, final selection, and supporting evidence, which attempt would now make you more successful?

Sunday School/Church

Wedding

Song Titles

Nursery Rhymes

Teenage Cruisin'

Mystery Box

❖ Gather enough opaque containers for each group of three or four students. The containers can be the same or different.

❖ Place one common household object in each container. The containers need not contain the same objects.

❖ Seal the containers so students are unable to open them or see inside.

❖ Pass the containers out to student groups. Provide the following directions:

    ❖ There is something inside each of these containers.

    ❖ You may not open it or damage the container in any way.

    ❖ As a group, you need to gather as much evidence as you can to determine what is inside your container.

    ❖ Once you gather the evidence, your group should make a claim as to what is inside the container.

    ❖ Write your claim with supporting evidence on the chart paper provided.

    ❖ Be ready to defend your claim to your peers.

❖ After an appropriate amount of time, student groups present their claim and evidence. The nonpresenting groups should listen politely, question critically, and offer suggestions to strengthen the evidence.

❖ If time permits, groups can gather additional evidence based on the suggestions provided.

❖ Teachers may or may not choose to allow groups to open the container at the end of the activity.

An alternative activity that is an intriguing experience for students involves using a microscope and projector. Show students common objects (for example, human hair, a penny, paper) and ask groups to make a claim on each object, providing evidence to support each claim. Can the group come up with a consensus? What if they can make only one claim based on the evidence? This will make a space in your classroom for argumentation and negotiation!

How Do I Get My Students to Negotiate Their Understanding?

In previous chapters, we talked about the classroom conditions that must exist for our students to think deeply and to question each other as well as their own learning. This work involves risk on the part of the student. Jot down some things that are currently in place in your classroom that support thinking and questioning. Consider: "How do my actions as the teacher support the negotiation of meaning by the learner?" For more information, see Chapter 5.

One way to begin this idea of argumentation and negotiation is to begin with something familiar to the students. Ask them to name their favorite children's story. If your students are older, you can ask them to write down a favorite quote from a book. Now, on the backside of that paper, ask the students to write down why they like this book or quote so much. Organize the students in groups of four to six and ask each member of the group to take a turn sharing his or her claim (favorite book or quote). The other members of the group discuss their thoughts on the student's choice. When the student in charge decides he or she has heard enough, she flips the page over and shares the personal evidence as the last comment, and the conversation moves to the next student. In this experience, the students have the opportunity to hear others make claims and evidence in relation to the original claim. This can also be a powerful strategy to transfer to a science investigation when appropriate.

An important tool in the SWH approach is the template to help students negotiate meaning (see Figure F.1). One way to get started using the template in your classroom is to use it with the "Mr. Xavier" murder mystery shared in Appendix E (and in Chapter 6). Begin by having the students read the story. Then, ask the students to fill in the template, individually at first. Next, ask them to share their thinking with a partner. Ask the pair to come forward with *one* agreed-upon claim. From there, put two pairs together and continue the pattern until the whole class is negotiating together and must bring one claim to the teacher. Be prepared: They will expect that then you will provide the correct answer!

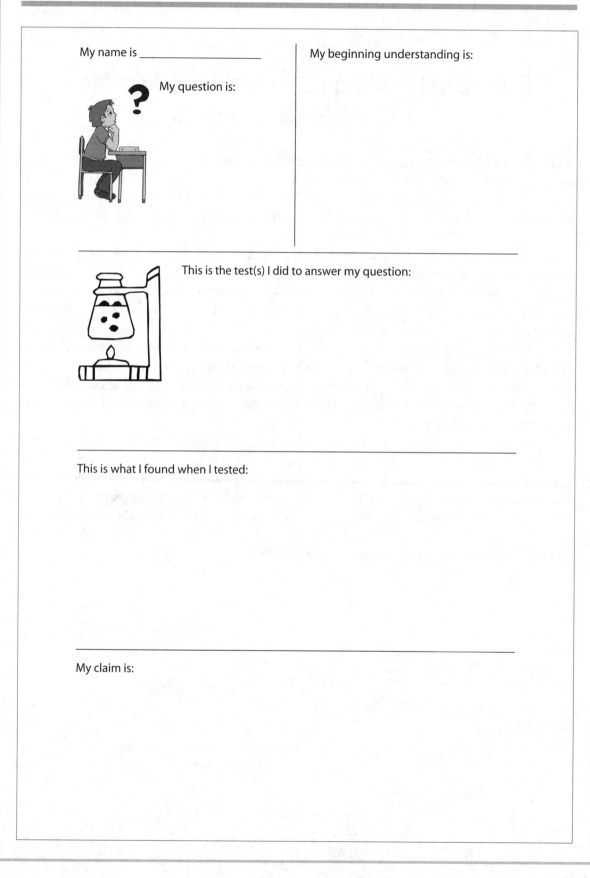

My name is _____

My question is:

My beginning understanding is:

This is the test(s) I did to answer my question:

This is what I found when I tested:

My claim is:

My evidence is:

_____

Other people say:

Internal Sources   External Sources

_____

Reflections:

My ideas have changed because:

My ideas haven't changed because:

How Do I Incorporate Literature into My SWH Units?

In the SWH process, we use literature in nearly every step of the process. Using the SWH Teacher Template, here are examples of how we incorporate both fiction and nonfiction in our classrooms.

Nonfiction Books

A plethora of great nonfiction books is available today. A comprehensive list would take many, many pages. Teachers might want to begin by examining books from some of our favorite authors: Kathryn Lansky, Patricia Lauber, and Seymour Simon. A few books that we have used as we begin units of study follow:

Books to Develop an Understanding of the Role of a Scientist:

❖ *Snowflake Bentley* (Jacqueline Briggs 1998)

❖ *Being a Scientist* (Shared Reading-Early Science Collection)

Book to Promote Discussion About Claims and Evidence:

❖ *Earthlets: As Explained by Professor Xargle* (Willis 1994)

Access to Print

In order to incorporate literature in science, it is helpful to have a classroom library containing both fiction and nonfiction books at a wide variety of reading levels. When students have easy access to books in their classrooms through classroom libraries, it is much easier to provide them with the opportunity to build background knowledge and look to the experts for answers to questions. Richard Allington (2005) recommends that every classroom should have 500 books and that these books should be evenly split between narrative and informational text. Additionally, he recommends that the books be evenly split between books that are on or near grade level and books that are below grade level.

One teacher, at the beginning of a unit on plants, found a wonderful text set—two crates full of books! The books fascinated the students, but the teacher was concerned because she had not yet found out what the students knew. At that moment, a lightbulb went off. She took the crates of books and spilled them in the middle of the group-time carpet. The children were asked to come join her at the carpet, sitting around the edges. She asked them each to grab a book, take a look, and talk to their neighbors about what they "see" in the books. The conversations were GRAND! The students discussed what made a good book and which ones were "too easy" because "I already know everything in this book!" They discussed text features and, yes, questions emerged and claims were made. Now the teacher had a very good idea what evidence needed to be collected. An added benefit is that the children became very familiar with this set of books right from the beginning of the unit, and they would return to them for information and ideas *daily*. And this all began with two crates of books!

Exploration of pre-instruction understanding	• Read aloud to activate prior knowledge; helps teacher to build background and to determine from discussions the misconceptions students might have about the big idea
Pre-laboratory activities	• Read aloud from selected passages to stimulate questions, build background, and develop curiosity • Provide books to students to look for answers to questions developed from concept map and question board • Provide books to students in order to provide an opportunity to raise additional questions
Participation in laboratory activity	• Books can be available as a reference to students as they are participating in the laboratory activity
Negotiation Phase I—writing personal meanings for laboratory activity	• Books available as reference tools
Negotiation Phase II—sharing and comparing data interpretations in small groups	• Books available as reference tools
Negotiation Phase III—comparing science ideas to text or other printed resources	• Wide variety of print and non-print materials (e.g., Internet sites) to provide students with the opportunity to check external sources for additional information
Negotiation Phase IV—individual reflection and writing	• Books available to help students see models of how authors write informational text
Exploration of post-instruction understanding	• Books available to help students see models of how authors write informational text

Figure G.1 *Incorporating literature into the SWH plan*

Read Aloud

Reading aloud to students is a great way to build background knowledge and to engage all students in the learning process. Students of all ages benefit from having teachers read aloud to them. When teachers read aloud from quality fiction or nonfiction books, they can help students ameliorate the deficit they may have in the content area being studied. See Chapter 5 for an example of a read aloud from *Owl Moon* by Jane Yolen.

Read Aloud Tool

Date: District/School:
Name, Grade Level:

Title of Book Used: Author:
Page(s):

Concepts Addressed from Science:

Language Arts Concepts and Processes Represented in the Text Selection:

Introduction to Book:

After Reading Discussion or Activity:

Adapted from Every Child Reads Materials, Iowa Department of Education 2005, Emily Calhoun, The Phoenix Alliance.

References

Allington, Richard. 2005. *What Really Matters for Struggling Readers*. Boston: Allyn & Bacon, 2nd Edition.

Ausubel, David P. 1968. *Educational Psychology: A Cognitive View*. New York: Holt, Rinehart and Winston.

Bazerman, Charles. 2008. *Handbook of Research on Writing: History, Society, School, Individual, Text*. New York: Lawrence Erlbaum Associates.

Bennett, Ben, Carol Rolheiser, and Laurie Stevahn. 1991. *Cooperative Learning: Where Heart Meets Mind*. Toronto: Educational Connections.

Calhoun, Emily. 1999. *Teaching Beginning Reading and Writing with the Picture Word Inductive Model*. Alexandria, VA: ASCD.

Calkins, Lucy M. 1994. *The Art of Teaching Writing*. Portsmouth NH: Heinemann.

———. 2001. *The Art of Teaching Reading*. New York: Longman.

Cambourne, Brian. 1987. *The Whole Story: Natural Learning and the Acquisition of Literacy in the Classroom*. Auckland, NZ: Ashton Scholastic.

Freire, Paulo. 1998. *Pedagogy of Freedom: Ethics, Democracy, and Civil Courage*. Lanham, MD: Rowman & Littlefield Publishers, Inc.

Friedman, Reva C., and Steven W. Lee, 1996. Differentiating instruction for high-achieving/gifted children in regular classrooms: A field test of three gifted education models. *Journal for Education of the Gifted*, 19(4), 405–36.

Fowler, Barbara. 1996. *Critical Thinking Across the Curriculum Project*. Longview Community College, Lees Summit, MO. Retrieved from the Internet August 30, 2007. http://mcckc.edu/longview/ctac/blooms.htm.

Gee, James P. 1996. *Social Linguistics and Literacies: Ideology in Discourses*. (2nd ed.). Philadelphia: Routledge/Farmer.

Goodman, Yetta M. 2003. *Valuing Language Study: Inquiry into Language for Elementary and Middle Schools*. Urbana, IL: National Council of Teachers of English.

Gowin, Dixie. 1981. *Educating*. Ithaca, NY: Cornell University Press.

Graves, Don, and Penny Kittle, 2005. *Inside Writing: How to Teach the Details of Craft*. Portsmouth, NH: Heinemann.

Hand, Brian, and Carolyn Keys, 1999. Inquiry investigation. *The Science Teacher*, 66(4), 27–29.

Jacqueline Briggs, M. M. 1998. *Snowflake Bentley*. Boston: Houghton Mifflin.

Klein, Perry D. 1999. Reopening inquiry into cognitive processes in writing-to-learn. *Educational Psychology Review*, 11(3), 203–70.

Kristo, R. A. 2003. *Making Facts Come Alive: Choosing & Using Quality Nonfiction*. (2nd ed.). Christopher-Gordon Publishers.

Lemke, Jay. 1990. *Talking Science: Language, Learning, and Values*. Norwood, NJ: Ablex.

Llewellyn, Douglas. 2001. *Inquire Within: Implementing Inquiry-Based Science Standards*. Thousand Oaks, CA: Sage Publications.

McLaughlin, Maureen, and Mary Beth Allen. 2002. *Guided Comprehension: A Teaching Model for Grades 3–8*. Newark, DE: International Reading Association.

Merriam, Eve. 1991. *The Wise Woman and Her Secret*. New York: Simon and Schuster Children's Publishing

Moss, Barbara. 2002. *Exploring the Literature of Fact: Children's Non-fiction Trade Books in the Elementary Classroom*. New York: The Guilford Press.

National Research Council. 1996. *National Science Education Standards*. Washington, D.C.: National Academy Press.

Norris, Steven P., and Linda M. Phillips, 2003. How literacy in its fundamental sense is central to scientific literacy. *Science Education*, 87, 224–40.

Northwest Regional Educational Laboratory. 2001. *Research on Writing: Classroom Questioning*. School Improvement Research Series.

Osborne, Jonathan, Shirley Simon, and Sibel Enduran. 2003. *Ideas, Evidence and Argument in Science (IDEAS)*. London: King's College.

Pearce, Charles 1999. *Nurturing Inquiry: Real Science for the Elementary Classroom*. Portsmouth, NH: Heinemann.

Pearson, P. David, and Gina Cervetti, 2005. Reading and writing in the service of acquiring scientific knowledge and dispositions: In search of synergies. A presentation given at the International Reading Association Annual Reading Research Convention, San Antonio, TX, April 30.

Piaget, Jean, and Barbel Inhelder. 1969. *The Psychology of the Child*. New York: Basic Books.

Reynolds, Peter H. 2004. *Ish*. Cambridge, MA: Candlewick Press.

Ruggieri, Denise. 2007. Chatter bugs. Retrieved from the Internet, December 12, 2007. http://adulted.about.com/od/icebreakers/a/chatterbugs.htm.

Saul, E. Wendy. 2004. *Border Crossing: Essays on Literacy and Science*. Newark, DE: International Reading Association/National Science Teachers Association.

Shared Reading—Early Science Collection. *Being A Scientist*. Madison, WI: Demco.

Showers, Beverly. 2006. Second Chance Reading Teaching Academy. Des Moines, IA. August.

Spandel, Vicki. 2004. *Creating Young Writers*. New York: Pearson Education.

Stotsky, Sandra. 1983. Research on reading/writing relationships: A synthesis and suggested directions. *Language Arts*, 60, 627–42.

Strike, Kenneth A. 1987. Toward a coherent constructivism. In J. Novak (Ed.), *Proceedings of the 2. Int. Seminar Misconceptions and Educational Strategies in Science and Mathematics, Vol. I*. Ithaca, NY: Cornell University, 481–89.

Tierney, Robert J., Anna Soter, John O'Flahavan, and William McGinley. 1989. The effects of reading and writing on thinking critically. *Reading Research Quarterly*, 24, 134–73.

Thacker, Jerry. 1991. *Thinking About Critical Thinking*. In Gough, D. (Ed.). *Thinking About Thinking*. Alexandria, VA: National Association of Elementary School Principals, 1991. (ED 327 980).

Vygotsky, Lev. 1962. *Thought and Language*. Cambridge, MA: The M.I.T. Press.

———. 1978. *The Mind in Society*. Cambridge, MA: Harvard University Press.

Willis, Jeane. 1994. *Earthlets: As Explained by Professor Xargle*. London: Puffin.

Wohlwend, Karen. 2004. Seeking the essential question. Whole Language Umbrella Conference, St. Louis, MO.

Index